SC CONFIDENCE MASTERY

How to Eliminate Social Anxiety, Insecurities, Shyness, and the Fear of Rejection

By Adam Rockman

WWW.EVOLVETOWIN.COM

Copyright 2016 By Adam Rockman – all rights reserved.

This document aims to provide reliable information in regards to the topics covered. Author and publisher are not liable for any consequences to engaging in any of the provided advice.

In no way is it legal to reproduce, duplicate, or transmit any part of this document in either electronic means or in printed format. Recording of this publication is strictly prohibited and any storage of this document is not allowed without written permission from the publisher. All rights reserved.

Contents

Chapter 1: Introduction to Social Confidence 1

Chapter 2: Should you Fake it Till you Make it? 49

Chapter 3: How to Quickly Get Into a Social Mood without Alcohol 69

Chapter 4: Real Happiness 79

Chapter 5: How to Develop Self-acceptance 114

Chapter 6: Accepting Anxious Feelings 143

Chapter 7: How to Overcome Social Anxiety 151

Chapter 8: Limiting Beliefs 168

Chapter 9: Giving Versus Taking 185

Chapter 10: Achieving your Social Confidence Goals 192

Chapter 11: Rejection 201

Chapter 12: How to Be Assertive 217

Chapter 13: Self Amusement 228

Chapter 14: Confident Communication Skills 243

Chapter 15: Your 10 Day Social Confidence Plan 263

Chapter 16: Conclusion 286

Chapter 1: Introduction to Social Confidence

"The problem with the world is that the intelligent people are full of doubts, while the stupid ones are full of confidence."
— **Charles Bukowski**

Zach is a 30 year old burger flipper at McDonalds. When he was younger he dreamt of becoming a comedian. He envied the comic's freedom to say whatever he wanted. He admired their ability to use timing and body language to pull in the audience's attention.

He has a great sense of humor. But every time he thinks of something funny to say in front of others he chokes and it won't come out because he's too worried about being judged. He has suffered from this anxiety since he was a child. He always wanted to break free of these fears and confidently express his humorous observations but every time he avoided an opportunity to face this anxiety he pushed himself farther away from his dream.

He is very lonely. He wants to make more friends, find a girlfriend and have better relationships with everyone. He is trying to find the courage to join a public speaking class but the idea of speaking in front of strangers still makes him panic. He's worried his shaky, quiet voice will be seen as weak and irritating.

Sometimes his friends invite him to social events. He refuses when he thinks of all the embarrassing scenarios he could suffer if he attends. His mind is a mess of contradictions. On one hand he wants to hide and never be bothered by potential embarrassment. On the other hand he wants to overcome these ridiculous fears and finally be able to articulate who he is to both himself and others. It's like driving a car and hitting the gas and brake at the same time.

For some people, social anxiety is so painful they are terrified to interact with anyone. Even asking directions or interacting with a cashier can be as scary as appearing nude on TV to fight a wild Grizzly bear. If that sounds like you then this book will push you to overcome barriers to a happy social life. If however you are already comfortable interacting with most people but want more friends, dates, and freedom from the fear of rejection and social scrutiny then this book can be even more valuable to you.

Zach hasn't become a successful comedian yet. But he did eventually find the courage to go to social events, start conversations, and after only a week of pushing himself he managed to tell a few jokes on stage at a local comedy club without stuttering like an idiot. He even received a few laughs and genuine applause.

Before Zach fixed some serious inner doubts he made a lot of mistakes in social situations. He spoke too quickly, too quietly, avoided eye contact and ended interactions before he had a chance to feel rejected.

He spent a few weeks enduring these uncomfortable interactions before he admitted it was his own behavior that needed to be adjusted. He trained himself to speak loudly, slowly, maintain proper eye contact and fixed a few other bad habits and his interactions clearly improved. People would talk to him. Sometimes he even had good interactions. This let him relax and he was less worried what the other person thought of him. This was especially true when he talked to an attractive woman. He desperately wanted her approval and it made him more nervous and scared of losing her. When she finally smiled, or somehow showed interest he finally felt like he could relax and be himself.

He was having some social success but he was still terrified of rejection. By mimicking confident body language he was like a malnourished kitten wearing the hide of a lion to impress others. It took a lot of time and honest confrontation with his fear and inner problems to see real progress. He used many of the techniques presented in this book to do that. He also worked on getting his life together. He started his own small business and lives off the profits.

As he started living more and more in abundance he lost that needy fear of rejection. He began providing positive emotions to others instead of depending on validation from others to feel good. As his life and opinion of himself changed so did his self-esteem. Social confidence became natural and people couldn't believe he was once a shy awkward virgin scared of rejection.

If you really want social confidence you will need to face your fears. You will need to break bad habits and think about why you developed them in the first place.

You will need to be honest with yourself.

That vulnerability will become a strength. You can fix the symptoms of social anxiety but if you haven't handled your deeper feelings of inadequacy people easily see through the fake façade. At least socially intelligent people usually do.

The following chapter in this book does indeed go in-depth on various social skills men of poise naturally use. A lot of people suggest you should fake it until you make it. They advise you to adopt confident looking body language, speak loudly and force yourself to hold eye contact. They theorize that eventually these habits will become your natural way of expressing yourself. That may be helpful but it is not enough. There are internal issues to resolve and pain to let go of before you can feel genuinely confident with others.

Has anything similar to this ever happened to you? You are at a party or night club and try to start a conversation with a cute stranger.

"Hey how much is a beer here?" You ask. Or maybe you gave a compliment on their appearance. However the other person just stares at you blankly with no reaction. Then with a look of disgust they turn their back and ignore you. Outside you might look calm, however internally you might not be feeling okay. All your fears have come true. You went to a social venue and somebody didn't like you. Somehow, not every person in the world was open to being your best friend.

How did this happen? Is something wrong with you? Aren't you flawless? Don't all people want to be close to you? Oh no! Somebody doesn't love you! The fact that the next few people you could have approached would have given you a great reaction is irrelevant. You needed to prove to yourself that every single person loves you! And you failed! There is no way to cope with this failure! It's time to give up on humanity and retreat to your hobbit hole and abstain from bathing for a few weeks while you live terrified of even making a simple phone call because it would mean talking to another human being who might judge you as unworthy.

That exaggerated consequence is exactly the baseless paranoia that leads many people to avoid social situations that would actually lead to developing confidence.

It's the fear of confronting the truth of their imperfection.

The fear that not everyone finds them attractive.

The fear of not being good enough. For some people this fear is so severe they are terrified of leaving their home and interacting with anyone.

You don't need to be loved by every person. You don't need everyone's approval. When you honestly express yourself some people will be closed minded or just be dealing with their own antisocial issues. But plenty of other people will be happy to meet and interact with you.

Often people will go to a social event, have one bad interaction and give up on meeting anyone else because they had their feelings hurt. Perhaps they should later spend time reflecting on their pain to see what they can learn from the experience. However, immediately giving up prevents them from experiencing numerous enjoyable experiences.

I once went to an event that I had been to many times previously. It's a very social event and it's always easy to start a friendly conversation with everyone there. I had just had great interactions with about a dozen people and then my friend and I approached another small group. I smiled and said something like, "Hi nice to meet you guys, I think we haven't talked to you yet." Everyone seemed friendly enough except one girl in the group who just gave a cold stare and demanded to know, "Why are you talking to me?" I was shocked at this rude response. I calmly explained that it was a social event and everyone had always been friendly and receptive until I'd met her. I tried to ask a few interesting questions but she refused to answer. I don't know why she was so angry. I forget the rest of the interaction, but I eventually stated that she doesn't seem to be in a social mood so probably shouldn't be at an event like this one. One of her friends apologized for her foul mood and they left.

Who knows what species of parasite crawled up her backside. There could have been all sorts of problems going on in her life. Or maybe she seriously misunderstood the nature of the event. I did nothing wrong and I was as polite as possible.

It shook me a bit because it was so unexpected. However I didn't let it ruin my night. I met a few more really interesting people and had a lot of fun. There was once a time I wouldn't have been able to handle it though. When I was socially inexperienced meeting an antisocial person like that could have devastated me. Now I just feel sorry for people like that because they aren't capable of having fun.

The socially anxious are terrified of experiences like that. The truth is those experiences help you grow. Facing them have helped me build confidence and made me a much better man. I now welcome these experiences because I know they help me level up.

You can't just live an isolated life hidden away from the dangers of running into obnoxious people who will reject you. It will only retard your growth and leave you stuck in an immature level of development. Don't run away from the lessons life is trying to teach you. The only result is an unlived life. You may somehow make it to your 100th birthday, but inside you will still be a child scared of growing up.

Imagine you become that old someday. Your life is about to end. You can feel it. You are lying in the bed you will die in. You are too weak to stand up. You can only lie there reflecting on your life. Think about the people you've met. Think about all your regrets. All the times you could have faced a fear but you didn't take action. Think about the places you wanted to visit but never did. Think about the people you never got to share your real feelings with. Think about the relationships you missed out on. Think about the relationships you stayed in out of fear. Think about all the opportunities you missed. Think about those several women who smiled at you in public but you didn't have the guts to start a conversation. Think about how you never faced your fears. Think about how every chance you got to change yourself you instead chose to take the lazy route and just stagnate instead of taking action. Think about all the experiences you wish you had.

You are dead. It's all over. All those missed chances for growth gone. You could have become a very confident person. But you gave up all the opportunities to develop confidence. It's time to say goodbye to this life that you never actually lived.

As you are leaving, you get a glimpse at how your life could have looked like if you had taken more action. You see yourself facing fears. It's painful, but eventually that version of yourself is happy and free, has lots of friends, and success in every area of life. How painful does it feel to know your life could have been completely different?

Now I have a surprise for you.

You can come back! It doesn't have to be like that! From this moment you can see social anxiety as an opportunity for growth. As you gain experience your life will change! You get another chance at life! Will you waste it this time too?

Your entire life is a result of the decisions you make. Make the decision to interact with the world no matter how awkward it may feel at times. When life presents the choice between growth and stagnation you know which to choose.

Social anxiety is a physical sensation that tempts you to hide from social interaction. The fear of rejection or fear of being judged is actually an opportunity to train yourself. When you have a chance to talk to someone but you are too scared to even say "hi" this avoidance only trains a habit of avoiding social interaction. However when you force yourself to talk to a new person it reinforces the belief that social interaction is easy.

Ironically social anxiety is often the very thing that leads to your rejection. When sociable people see you are closed off and afraid it is unattractive. People in an open positive mood gravitate towards each other. The goal of this book is to teach you how to get into that positive social mood.

You can have fun.

You can relax.

You can develop a sense of humor and enjoy talking to lots of people. To do this, requires immersion in social situations and learning from your experiences.

To make this immersion as educational as possible below is a summary of ten keys to the process of mastering social confidence.

We will dive deeper into each of these throughout the book.

It will be helpful to write them down and formulate your own plan for each key.

1. Practice confident body language
2. Immerse yourself in social situations
3. Keep a record of your interactions
4. Say yes to things that make you uncomfortable
5. Surround yourself with high quality friends
6. Meditate
7. Introspection
8. Record yourself.
9. Be open to everyone
10. Make plans and invite people

1. Practice confident body language

We will cover more details on confident body language in the next chapter. We've already seen that working on body language, while beneficial, may be similar to treating symptoms but not the disease. If you cultivate confidence it would instantly fix most of your timid body language anyway. It could resolve stuttering, poor eye contact, and other indications of fear.

With that said, it is still valuable to be aware of what confident body language looks like. You might be able to lie with your words but your body language almost always says exactly what you are feeling. So pay attention to how you present yourself to the world.

2. Immerse yourself in social interactions

People often don't like state changes. When you wake up, you might not feel like getting out of bed. When you are awake you might stay up late because you don't feel like sleeping. When you are social and having fun it's easier to move to the next interaction. However if you haven't had a real conversation with another person for a few weeks then you might not feel ready to immerse yourself in daily social interactions.

It's completely natural to resist socializing if you haven't done so recently. You can start with some simple events where people will likely be very friendly and easy to talk to.

An easy option is searching for events in your area on a site such as Meetup.com. This site has activities for any kind of topic or activity you might be interested in. They have meet ups to play board games, practice languages, play sports, discuss books and current events, yoga, hiking trips and anything you can think of! You can even find self-improvement groups you can join for support in your confidence building efforts.

In my experience Meetup events are completely stress free. It's easy to talk to everyone attending as you are all there for a mutual purpose. Meetups are an easy choice for finding opportunities to socialize and develop your confidence.

Maybe you still have the fear inside before you arrive. Maybe you are worried people will judge your awkwardness. But that doesn't matter. The way it works is you get the courage after you do what you are afraid of. Not before.

Eventually you will get used to various social environments and you can go to bigger events and social venues by yourself.

In fact it may be much more beneficial for you to go out alone. Force yourself to engage the social environment without needing a friend by your side. When you are with a friend it's easy to focus on talking with each other instead of conversing with new people. It's a convenient excuse for avoiding the discomfort of new experiences. By going out alone you get to challenge yourself to meet new people and gain experiences that will empower you.

3. Keep a record of your interactions

When you devote time to immersing yourself in social interaction it's helpful to keep a record of your experiences.

This is important because it helps you reflect on what you've learned and what you should do differently in the future. You don't need to write down every detail of every interaction. You only need to spend about 10 minutes a day taking some notes on 1 or 2 interactions you had during the day.

Here are the key points you might write down:

1. What happened?
2. How did I feel?
3. How did I react?
4. How can I improve next time?

It may sound simple but this exercise is crucial to developing social awareness. By writing about your awkward, embarrassing, emotionally painful experiences you can be honest with yourself about their impact on you instead of hiding your pain and pretending you are flawless.

It also helps to reinforce helpful lessons.

It's a practice in honestly embracing reality.

Conversely, if you have endless positive experiences but never reflect on them you are also missing out on opportunities to learn and improve.

4. Say yes to things that make you uncomfortable

Only refuse something you know to be dangerous. Such as kicking a wild lion in the face. In that situation you know there could be deadly consequences for you. However, in most social situations fear is not proportionate to actual danger. If you see a cute stranger, feel the urge to say "hi," but the only reason you don't do it is that uncomfortable feeling in your gut scaring you out of it, then it is even more reason to do it. Because you should prove to yourself it is completely safe. The worse that could happen is she isn't in a social mood and walks away. Even if she shouts a rude reply, it doesn't take anything away from who you are. Talk to a few more people and you'll eventually find someone much friendlier to chat with.

The only thing preventing you from starting an enjoyable interaction in that scenario was fear. When the only reason you don't want to do something is because you're scared, then you should do it!

Here is an analogy which highlights how ridiculous this is. Pretend you are a child. You are very shy and don't want to go to a new school because you are worried you won't make friends. You are worried the teacher will yell at you. You cry and beg your parents to let you stay home. And they do let you stay home forever and never go to school. And every time you beg your parents to let you avoid social interaction they submit to your requests. You never need to buy something in a store, make phone calls, ask directions, or do anything that involves interacting with another human being. What kind of person do you think you would turn into?

Of course, you would most likely turn into an extremely timid person terrified of talking to anyone. Mostly because of lack of experience and the habit of avoiding experiences you assume to be scary. The more experiences you avoid the scarier you think people are.

In this scenario, do you think your parents did a good job of raising you? Didn't protecting you from potentially uncomfortable experiences do more harm than good? Sure you were able to avoid some embarrassing moments but at what cost? You are left with no social experience and never resolved that social anxiety. Eventually you were crushed under its weight.

Isn't a parent like that completely irresponsible? You could have learned so much if your parent had forced you to do the most emotionally painful choice. You would have gained numerous experiences that forced you to grow.

Hopefully you see the point of this analogy already. It's up to you to be your own parent and force yourself to make the best decisions for your growth especially when it's uncomfortable. When you allow yourself to chicken out of an opportunity to grow up you are only being irresponsible with your own life and happiness.

5. Surround yourself with a variety of high quality friends

Perhaps you have heard the idea that you are the average of the people you spend the most time with. The people around you definitely influence who you become. So it's important to be aware of the impact your friends have on you.

Some people say you should kick all the negative people out of your life and surround yourself with positive people. The idea is that negative people are constantly complaining and whining and it makes you feel bad. Eventually you could become infected by their toxic personalities.

That is often true. Some people just have a nasty personality its best to avoid. But this doesn't mean all negativity should be ignored. Often your friends criticize you because they hope to see you succeed, not because they want to tear you down. While criticism may on the surface appear negative, it can actually be very positive when the intention behind it is to help you.

This is why you should spend time with people who have different viewpoints from your own. When everyone around you is always confirming your biases that is also an impediment to growth.

It's possible you've never contemplated what kind of friend you'd like to have in your life.

Many friendships just form over a few conversations and it just seems to work out. These relationships are formed from the investments we make in each other. Unfortunately, you might end up with friends who take more value from you than they give back. You don't need to cut people out of your life if they have traits you admire. But you can still find more people who are exactly like what you want to become. You can find confident friends. You can find friends you want to learn from. You can find friends you would really enjoy spending time with.

6. Meditate

Calming the chatter of your mind isn't the only benefit of regular meditation. As long as you can commit to a long term meditation habit you will experience many benefits. Studies have shown that mediation can change the brain in ways that make you less prone to anxiety and stress.

What I really like about mediation is it allows me to ignore all the past and present bullshit of life. I can tune out all the distractions. I become present to the moment. At least that's my goal. Sometimes a certain topic will keep repeating in the mind. You don't need to control your thoughts. You just need to observe them. And ask yourself, "Why in the world did I think that?"

Meditation is also helpful to reigning in uncontrollable negative emotional reactions. For most people negative reactions are automatic. You've likely observed people going nuts over the smallest thing. I've seen people angrily shouting expletives for the pettiest reasons. Such as a fast food restaurant being out of an item they wanted. They lose their agency. They shout and swear. The world didn't fulfill their desires and they want revenge.

By quietly disconnecting from the petty disappointments of life we can calm the mind. With regular meditation the body gets a chance to take a break from negative thoughts that drain energy and the body's resources.

Let's imagine your body is a car. When you allow your emotions to take control of your behavior it's like letting the car drive itself. Where is the driver? You should be driving your car. You should be consciously choosing your thoughts and emotions. However this can be a challenge when we are stuck in the habit of letting the car drive itself. This means that if for example you are angry, that emotion will dictate your behavior. However, if you can maintain a calmer state of mind, you can still react appropriately without letting the negative emotions impede your judgement. With practice meditation can help alleviate emotional overreactions.

In 2010 an article in the Journal of Consulting and Clinical Psychology surveyed 39 studies of meditation based therapy on general social anxiety and other conditions, mostly mood related. The total sample of participants included 1140 people. In a majority of these studies people did experience relief from stress, anxiety, and related conditions with the help of regular meditation. The conclusion of this article was that meditation *"is a promising intervention for treating anxiety and mood problems in clinical populations."*

The science indicates meditation helps with anxiety, stress and social intelligence. It's connected to diminishing lonely negative thoughts. It's also a vital part of accepting the internal struggles that lead to social anxiety and unnecessary fear.

You don't need these thousands of studies to prove to you meditation has tangible benefits. You only need to try it to see for yourself. It takes an effort to start a regular mediation habit but eventually you will see results.

There are many established benefits to meditation:

- Enhances your emotional well-being
- Decreases anxiety and depression
- Improves resilience to pain and adversity
- Increases optimism
- Improves mood
- Increases mental strength and focus
- Improves memory
- Better creative thinking
- Helps you ignore distractions
- Improves immune system
- Reduces blood pressure

If you feel resistance to the idea of meditation, please write a list of why you don't want to do it. If you are feeling too lazy to write a list, at least think about it for a moment. Why can't you spend 5 minutes a day alone with your thoughts? You must be able to find 5 minutes of time to yourself each day.

The more excuses you have for avoiding meditation the more you need it in your life! Because more excuses indicates you are addicted to external stimuli and are having trouble taking a break. It's ok to relax for a few minutes to an hour of very relaxing meditation. The world will still be there when you get back.

When you first start meditating it may in fact feel boring. You are just sitting there and nothing is happening.

But that is exactly the point.

You may have become addicted to always having something to do. Always having a phone in your hands, a computer on your lap, a song to listen to, or some other form of entertainment.

While enjoyable, these are distractions. When you can train yourself to resist these temptations, you will simultaneously train willpower and emotional control.

Even after people acknowledge how beneficial meditation is, why do they still refuse to develop this habit? The simple answer is they are already addicted to their daily routines. They dismiss meditation because they don't yet believe in the benefits.

Meditate daily for a month before you decide it's worthwhile or not. You don't need to take the word of regular meditators or the research backing up the benefits, you can simply try out meditation for yourself if you don't have a regular meditation habit yet.

Meditation would take away a chunk of time most people would rather spend on their cravings for other stimulation, such as TV, food, and internet browsing. Some say meditation is just a waste of time. But this is only because they have never practiced meditation themselves and haven't yet experienced the benefits.

For them, meditation has not yet been recognized as the reward it really is.

With meditation you have a chance to break free from your habits and emotions.

To get started you simply need to find your motivation for building this worthwhile habit.

There are many different kinds of meditation. In the most basic form you sit or lie down in a comfortable position, close your eyes, and pay attention to your thoughts. Don't try to control your thoughts, just let them go wherever they want and pay attention to what is happening.

This is the basic process of developing mindfulness. You don't need to memorize some complicated meditation techniques to experience the benefits of meditation. However when you realize the benefits of basic meditation it might be helpful for you to research more advanced meditation practices to help you on your journey of improving yourself.

Basic Meditation:

There are many different types of meditation. Each with variations that are supposed to help alleviate different burdens or help you improve in different ways.

There are many forms of meditation. Some are overly complicated. Some authors write a long list of 50 or more steps for what to imagine, feel, and how to breathe at which point in the meditation. I'm sure some of those forms of meditation with a long series of steps can in fact be very effective for their goals.

Go ahead and look for information on those types of meditations if they interest you. I like how having a series of steps during meditation such as breathing and visualizations can distract you from how much time is passing, which is great if you are still worried about being disconnected from your usual routine.

However you don't need to over contemplate it. Meditation is very simple and so here I want to provide some simple suggestions for how to benefit from usual meditation.

It's important to set regular times to your meditation practice each day as this helps you to associate that time with your meditation practice. As mentioned I recommend adding meditation to your morning and bedtime routines.

Commit to at least 5 minutes each time.

This will make it easy to remember. It can be relaxing to stretch first to loosen your muscles and tendons. If you can, find a place that you can devote to meditation, such as a certain chair or comfortable spot in a room. This will help you to associate this location with the relaxing states of meditation.

1. **Sit in a comfortable position.**
   (Unless you want to challenge yourself with an uncomfortable position, your choice.) Take a few slow deep breaths. Many recommend breathing through your nose if you can. Though it isn't necessary.

2. **Bring your attention to your body.**
   Pay attention to your senses. What do you feel? Slowly shift your attention from your feet up through the rest of your body. This is to transition your mind into a more relaxed state by first paying attention to how your body is sensing the world and how you are feeling.

3. **Observe your thoughts.**
   Once you are relaxed you can move on to the next step. You don't need to try and control your thoughts. Some forms of meditation do however involve the practice of developing focus. During those forms of meditation you would imagine some shape or image and focus only on that for as long as possible. Whenever your mind is distracted you bring your thoughts back to the image you are focusing on.

That is effective at developing focus and you may try it if you like, however it is not necessary to experience the many benefits of meditation.

Simply being aware of your thoughts as your minds drifts is enough. When your mind wanders, just tell yourself its ok and come back to relaxing. There is no need to resist any thought or sensation. Just let it all happen.

Pay attention to your breathing. Breathe in, breathe out. Don't try to control it, just let it happen naturally.

Don't stress yourself out about not seeing results immediately. It can be tempting to dismiss meditation if you only try it once or twice. However enough people have experienced significant psychological shifts as a result of daily meditation within as short of time as a month that it is highly recommended.

Observe how simple yet effective meditation is. You don't need to make it any more complicated than you like. If you aren't meditating regularly yet you won't know what benefits you could be missing out on until you try.

Advanced Meditation

Meditation is easy.

You just sit down, close your eyes, and listen to your mind talk with itself. Pay attention to the thoughts and be curious about where the thoughts and feelings are coming from.

Your basic meditation sessions may last anywhere from 10 minutes to half an hour and then you come out of it at least a bit more relaxed and ready to tackle life's responsibilities.

But I want to share with you a more advanced form of meditation that can train you for reinterpreting pain and various frustrations in life especially when it comes to social anxiety and the fear of rejection.

But first, contemplate the following question for a moment. What would happen if you had a completely pain free life? Maybe you were born with that condition where your pain receptors don't work. Well that's a cool super power isn't it!? You can fall down, break bones, get punched in the face, and none of it will hurt!

There would be damage of course, and many accidents as you were sure of the effects of any action you take. But at least you won't be able to feel it.

Then one day, a doctor tells you, *"Hey buddy, we've developed a new treatment that can turn on all your dormant pain receptors! You would finally be able to feel pain!"*

You decide to give it a try. Of course it's successful. You tap the back of your hand gently on the wall to test out your new ability and think to yourself, **"wow, so this is pain."** But that wasn't a real test, your pain receptors haven't even been engaged yet. Then later you are cutting some vegetables and accidently cut your finger a little. You suddenly scream in agony. *"Oh shit I cut myself! I'm dying!"* You fall to the floor. Tears flowing out of your eyes as you can't control your reaction.

Pain wasn't a part of your reality before. In fact pain doesn't need to be part of our reality. We have the ability to feel pain because it prevents us from doing stupid things that would damage ourselves. The role of pain is usually to indicate to us when there is a problem.

It wasn't even a deep cut. Your finger is barely bleeding, but because you never felt pain before you have no reference for the level of pain you can actually endure.

This metaphor applies to every kind of discomfort. If you are focused on avoiding pain, then you are resisting the present moment.

Pain is resistance to your current situation. All discomfort is resistance to your current situation. So instead of resisting, you should accept the present moment. By accepting your situation, you no longer interpret it as painful, uncomfortable or annoying. It is that interpretation that makes it painful.

That is why in this form of meditation you sit completely still for at least one hour. Sit in a comfortable position and stay there. Don't move at all for as long as you can. See how long you can stand complete stillness before the aches and itches in your body prevent you from continuing.

If you feel an itch don't scratch it. Just accept the itch. You may be surprised to find that within a minute or two most itches will just disappear on their own.

If any part of your body begins to ache, resist the urge to change positions. Accept the feelings you feel. Though uncomfortable you will survive.

This kind of meditation teaches you to accept reality no matter how it is. In fact, it teaches you to reinterpret discomfort as not being uncomfortable at all. This trains you to accept adversity, annoyances and a bit of pain. This is the super power you should really want. It's so much better than the inability to feel pain at all.

So how long can you endure of this type of meditation? Most people seem to be barely able to endure 10 minutes. They are used to resisting discomfort and avoiding pain. It's a useful survival strategy. However it's often much more uncomfortable than it needs to be.

Most annoyances in your life don't need to affect your emotions as much as they do. So you are late for work? So what? Be late. It's just a job. So your boss yelled at you for being late? So what? Assure him you won't be late again, make an effort to be on time and move on with your life. Why does it need to stress you out?

There must be more examples like that in your life. Minor annoyances that you interpret as uncomfortable and constantly resistant. That resistance is what makes you feel negative emotions. Those negative emotions drain your body of nutrients essential to producing the neurotransmitters that provide positive emotions.

This translates to less fear of rejection and a more solid confidence in yourself as your emotions begin to come from yourself rather than other people.

How long you can endure this kind of meditation?

5 Minutes – Did you even try?

You give up easily when facing a challenge. You are easily frustrated when things don't go your way. You may lie to yourself and say you can sit here for an hour if you really wanted to, but the first time your nose really starts itching you are scratching hard. You might also tell yourself that one itch you scratched is a freebie and thus didn't count. So you refuse to start over.

10 Minutes - Average

Sometimes you give up on new things when you feel it doesn't suit you. But at least you give a real effort. You really wanted to meditate in complete stillness for an hour, and you managed to get past a few small itches. You can get through some challenges that other people whine about. However some big challenges require you to make a bigger effort to actually achieve success.

30 Minutes – Experienced Meditator

Maybe you haven't been meditating for years yet, but you may have been practicing meditation daily for at least 2 weeks. You are starting to realize you can stay calm in some situations that previously annoyed you. However your habits of resisting discomfort keep coming back. Eventually you will give up when the pain is too much.

1 hour – Yoda

You have more than a few weeks of meditation experience. You might be a bit neurotic about training yourself to resist pain. You are more honest with yourself than many people. You are able to overcome many difficulties but you can at least admit to yourself when something becomes too challenging for you. You also start to feel more energized no matter what discomfort is present in your life.

2 hours - Superman

If you can sit completely still and resist the urge to move at all for 2 hours then you are definitely starting to feel some changes happening within you. Any discomfort you feel in your chest may start to loosen up and you can actually feel this happening. You are becoming more sociable and tolerant of previously annoying nonsense. You have accomplished a few great things in your life, but there is much more you dream about accomplishing. Your challenges are numerous, so choose that ones you are more passionate about.

4 hours – Buddha

If you can do this for 4 hours you might be enlightened. You will definitely experience something. You will also find you are becoming much more positive than before.

8 hours – Master of the Universe

Congratulations. You may be in complete control of your emotions. Nothing bothers you. Luckily you can still behave appropriately depending on the situation since you are still a human being interacting with other people. But the discomforts that used to trouble you are seen for the events they really are.

I recommend trying this form of advanced meditation after you have been practicing regular mediation for at least 2 weeks. Though I'm not your boss so go ahead and test yourself to see how long you can last.

After you can handle normal meditation for 20 minutes a day then aiming for an hour of advanced meditation several times a week will likely benefit you. It is of course a habit that works best over time. The longer you have spent practicing the more benefit it gives you. The more you are able to accept the present moment without judging. But it takes time to cultivate these things as meditation rewires your brain. Meditation alone won't cure your social anxiety. You also need to take action and get yourself into social situations. With practice meditation will help you stay centered when you take action and resist the negative emotional reactions that tempt you to shy away from confidently expressing yourself.

7. Introspection

We learn from experience and mistakes. No matter how awkward or embarrassing, many of these experiences can become valuable lessons in self-improvement instead of sources of shame. People are terrified of experiences they don't need to be afraid of. A shy guy is scared to talk to new people. Not for any logical reason. He just has an unexplainable fear of approaching new people. When he does find an ounce of courage to start a conversation he might make awkward or needy statements. He might display weak body language. He might stutter and avoid eye contact. However these are all learning opportunities. The only real mistake would be in not learning from these experiences and making an effort to improve his social skills.

Unfortunately it's possible to pass up opportunities for growth if you never reflect on your experiences. Research indicates that thinking about what you've been through and asking yourself what it means and how to improve is usually prerequisite for learning. Think of it like this. There must have been times you've sat in a class taught by a teacher you considered boring. His lessons may have been very informative but if you only passively listened to what was taught in class you likely didn't remember much of the material. You might also have memories of a teacher you found entertaining or you were very interested in the subject of the class. In that instance, you would be actively thinking about the topic, you would be forming questions in your mind and actually learning something.

Life experience is the same way. You can choose to be a passive observer and never learn anything from what's been thrown at you, or you can learn how to anticipate it and dodge.

Reflecting on your life experiences takes you from passive observation to understanding. If you understand your mistake its more likely you will make a plan to resolve it. Otherwise you might keep making the same mistake.

When you are in a social situation at work, school, event or party focus on the moment. Meet some people and practice expressing yourself honestly. Afterwards ask yourself:

"What did I do well?"

"What can I improve?"

This helps you make incremental progress towards improving your ability to express yourself and overall confidence in social situations.

This next point may be uncomfortable to accept. Even more importantly, reflection forces you to challenge your assumptions about reality. You may be forced to face uncomfortable truths that you don't want to accept. For example, many socially inexperienced men love to complain that women are all superficial and only date handsome rich men. Some women may in fact be this way but there are plenty of exceptions to this. I've seen lots of short balding guys of average to little wealth attracting lots of stunning women through their confidence and social skills alone. But the socially inexperienced guy is blind to that reality. His confirmation bias only allows him to see the women dating the good looking guys. This way he can maintain this false concept as an excuse to avoid self-improvement.

But what would happen if he had a more open mind? What if when faced with immense evidence to the contrary of his view he asked himself it was really ALWAYS true? Perhaps he would be open to the possibility that it was his social skills that were the major hindrance to his failure to find a girlfriend. Perhaps he would eventually give up on the negative belief that, "Women hate me because I'm ugly!" Even if you are ugly, I think women hate you because your negative personality makes people uncomfortable not the excuses you tell yourself to avoid confronting your flaws.

The point is to be open to questioning your ideas of the world. This opens you up to many possibilities.

In the scenario above the man with a pessimistic view of his dating life could realize he has the potential to develop his social skills and share life with some incredible people if he only believed it were possible instead of assuming nobody would ever want to socialize with him because of his below average appearance.

It's not only helpful to reflect on your mistakes.

It's also beneficial to reflect on your achievements and remind yourself what you've done well in social situations.

Even when you do make mistakes you can frame it very positively as a learning opportunity.

8. Record yourself.

If you've never video recorded yourself it can be uncomfortable at first to see and hear yourself. You may realize you have some bad habits you weren't aware of. If you can, record yourself talking with another person.

When you watch it pay attention to the volume and tone of your voice, eye contact, posture. Listen for any odd verbal ticks or indications of nervousness. Ask yourself why you felt that way in that moment.

This exercise forces you to confront nervous body language and bad habits that usually can be corrected with practice.

Record yourself in this manner several times over a few months and you will likely see a difference in your ability to express yourself more confidently.

9. Be open to everyone

Most people you meet won't become your friend. That doesn't mean you need to ignore potential value they could add to your life and that you could add to theirs.

In some venues you will notice needy individuals who are only interested in socializing with certain people. If it is at a night club it may be a needy guy who only talks to women and refuses to befriend her male friends and toxically sees them as "obstacles." Or if it is a more formal setting people might only be interested in meeting wealthy individuals with social status and completely ignore the penniless entrepreneur even though he is a highly interesting man with a lot of value to offer.

As you can see, this is a very selfish, needy, value taking frame of mind. When you have a goal it can be tempting to focus only on the people that can help you achieve it and ignore all the other opportunities for human connection. But you are missing out. In fact, you don't know what opportunities you could be missing out on if you act in such a selfish way. The guy in the night club could have talked to some overweight ladies, and then attractive girls could have seen him having fun and socializing with anyone, not just focused on extracting a target. Providing value is very attractive. Or maybe those overweight ladies had some cute friends. The snobs at the formal get together lost an opportunity to invest in the entrepreneur who later became a billionaire. You don't know what opportunities you are missing by being so closed minded and focused on exactly what you want.

Real social confidence should involve being willing to interact with anyone. It doesn't mean you always need to though.

Some people just can't relax and are intimidated by stress free people with social skills. However in most social situations it should be acceptable to interact with most people. In fact, it should also be enjoyable.

If you limit the kinds of people you interact with it will likely lead to frustration. Because that limitation you place on yourself causes unnecessary stress.

You may think you aren't cool enough to talk to an interesting person you'd like to meet. But you'll never know if they are willing to talk to you or not unless you try. Conversely you may think someone isn't interesting enough to talk to.

Many people only seem boring on the surface. Even sufferers of social anxiety. But once you get them relaxed and comfortable they can willingly share their humor and individuality.

Being open to new people, ideas, and experiences expands your intellectual capacity. Instead of only talking to people who look and think like you it can be an intriguing experience to interact with people with vastly different world views than your own.

One fear in social situations is that you might have an opinion or belief that conflicts with the person you are talking to. This could result in an uncomfortable confrontation in which the other person says you are wrong or insults you for your belief. Instead of fearing that scenario learn to embrace it. Be happy when it happens. Maybe you and the other person involved have something to teach each other.

Being open to others without limitations diminishes prejudices, makes you more optimistic, and has been shown to significantly decrease stress. This is because you aren't constantly afraid people will threaten you with their different way of thinking or living.

Possibly the most significant benefit to openness to everyone is that you gain incredibly valuable social experience. Instead of worrying what to do in a variety of situations you will know exactly what to do because you've already been in that situation many times before. Whether is a pleasurable or annoying situation you will already be prepared to handle it.

You could read 100 amazing books about developing confidence and not understand how to do it. However when you openly embrace and handle an immense variety of social situations it will fundamentally change you.

After interacting with people from a wide range of backgrounds and temperaments you won't be as scared of social situations as before. If you reflect on these experiences you will realize they are even more valuable than any book could ever articulate to you. That solid understanding based on actual experience is essential to developing genuine confidence.

10. Make plans and invite people

When you've started going to more social events, reflecting on your experiences, and meeting people you are interested in getting to know better it may be time to turn your new acquaintances into friends or more.

Socially successful people don't only sit and wait for invitations to hang out. They make plans and carve reality to their liking.

Think of an activity you would genuinely like to do with a few new friends.
Some examples:
- Drinking / clubbing
- Karaoke
- Paintball
- Beach volleyball
- Surfing
- Any sport
- Billiards
- Dinner at a theme restaurant
- Potluck dinner party at your house
- Picnic
- Board games
- Video games
- Hiking
- Biking
- Start a group on meetup.com and host meetups

It doesn't need to be elaborate. It could simply be dinner with a few of your new friends. You can have a great conversation and if things are going well have a plan for where to invite people after the meal.

When you start organizing events such as this people see you as a leader and they will start asking you to hang out. They will want to be invited to the next fun get together you organize. As long as people are having fun and enjoy your company it should be easy to gradually develop a regular group of people you can hang out with anytime. This shouldn't be much of an issue if you have been following a majority of the advice in this book for at least a few weeks.

Taking responsibility for social situations will be a huge boost to your confidence in social situations as well. Instead of worrying about what other people think of you, it's more likely your new acquaintances will be anxious about impressing you. After all, they want to hang out with you and meet your other interesting friends.

Obviously that is the ideal and life isn't always that simple. You might be the most sociable and fun person but it's difficult to make connections with interesting people you meet because they are too busy with their own plans. However this is no excuse to dismiss taking action in this area of your life. Maybe the people you invite will already have plans. Interesting people often have busy social lives already. That doesn't mean they are completely uninterested in hanging out with you. they may legitimately be busy. So spend a few weeks busy with your own plans. Have fun, meet and date new people, go on more adventures, read more books, live the life you want to live. And then the next time you invite someone to hangout it might be easier.

Thank you for purchasing this book!

As a surprise bonus, I want to offer you another book completely free!

100 Books Every Man Should Read is not just a list of books. It is a syllabus for self-growth and evolution. It covers the best books in every area men should be familiar with. Such as relationships, social skills, leadership, and much more.

Go to Evolvetowin.com to receive your free copy now.

Chapter 2: Should you Fake it Till you Make it?

"The world is full of people who are trying to purchase self-confidence, or manufacture it, or who simply posture it. But you can't fake confidence, you have to earn it. If you ask me, the only way to do that is work. You have to do the work."
— Russ Harris, The Confidence Gap: From Fear to Freedom

Maybe some people really do have psychological issues that prevent reinforcement of social habits that develop confidence. On the other hand it's also true many people latch onto that possibility as an excuse to avoid real change. Their identity becomes "the guy with social anxiety." And accepting that identity prevents change that could have been possible. Because if they change they can't have that identity anymore!

Facing social situations can be very uncomfortable. However there are plenty of people who were originally extremely awkward who developed confidence through practice and immersion in social situations. They chose to accept responsibility for their happiness and confidence. They struggled through a lot of failure, pain and rejection but each experience contained lessons that helped them level up. I've met a lot of these people and something they all have in common is they refused to accept that social anxiety was permanent.

It may take a lot of work to fix bad habits and face fears. Later we will dive deeper into how to really resolve the issues that make you afraid of what other people think of you and how to easily relax in social interactions.

First however we will talk about what confidence looks like. You can try to copy it, but it will feel more natural when you are actually feeling confident. If you've read some books on body language you will recognize some of this advice. If you are socially experienced you might roll your eyes and say a lot of it is common sense. However many people don't realize they are making mistakes in these areas. They automatically engage in awkward shy behavior as a defense and don't realize how it makes others perceive them.

For example, sometimes people have a weak handshake that feels like holding a live squid. It's uncomfortable, betrays their lack of confidence and is often accompanied by poor eye contact. Maybe nobody ever had the heart to criticize these people.

But they need to know that they could give a better handshake to improve their first impression.

Obviously mastering a proper handshake won't automatically make you completely confident. Your body language reveals your intentions and real feelings. Your eyes, tone of voice, and word choice can signal you are afraid of rejection and worried what people think of you.

Your posture, gestures, eye movements, facial expressions and voice are constantly revealing information about what's going on inside you. You might be able to lie with your words but body language is much more direct.

Although we've mentioned several times now that it's more important to work on your inner confidence than to fix the outward signs of nervousness there are important benefits to working on your body language.

Studies have shown that body language does in fact impact your physiology. You may have heard that even if you feel like crap smiling will make you feel better. The theory is that the smile is already associated with positive feelings and neurotransmitters such as serotonin which makes you feel great. When you smile it triggers the release of serotonin in the brain. In much the same way confident body language triggers neurotransmitters, adrenaline, and testosterone which impacts your mood.

It helps you to relax and feel more confident in social interactions. Conversely if you engage in nervous body language it only reinforces the feelings and brain chemistry of someone who lacks confidence.

So how should we develop confident body language?

Smile

Smiling slows the heart, lowers stress and releases endorphins that diminish the stress hormone cortisol.

Normally people smile and laugh when something is humorous or enjoyable.

At that moment you forget about your worries of the future and embarrassing memories.

You forget that sometimes you can be awkward and don't have something cool to add to the conversation. For a moment you can feel like yourself.

By smiling you tap into that mindset of being present to the moment. Stand in front of the mirror and smile at yourself for a minute or two after you wake up in the morning.

When you are reading this book or working on any task, you can take a moment to smile.

Notice how it makes you feel.

You might not become instantly full of joy, but it's likely you will feel at least a little better.

Smiling at other people can be even more therapeutic.

When they smile back how do you feel?

Try it and realize that you can positively impact the emotions of others and you will likely feel good too. Unless of course you are living in a haze of negativity and even if someone gives you a smile you assume they have evil intentions.

If that's the case then don't worry, there is still hope even for you.

Pay attention to your Posture

Good posture is not only healthier but it also makes you look and feel more confident. Sit with your back straight and entire back to the chair. Keep your feet on the floor. Bend your knees at a right angle. When you stand imagine a rope going through your spine and coming out the top of your head pulling you up. When you stand straight with your shoulders back and your head high you look confident.

It might be helpful to ask people if your posture looks good. Look out for these signs of habitual poor posture. You might suffer from anterior pelvic tilt with pulls your lower back forward. Another common posture issue is forward head in which your head protrudes in front of your body instead of sitting straight above your shoulders. Proper posture and some other exercises can fix those issues.

Eye Contact

Eye contact is a sign of confidence and familiarity. Too much eye contact can be aggressive, too little demonstrates fear or lack of interest in the other person. If eye contact makes you uncomfortable start practicing it with people you know. Eventually you can start practicing with everyone you meet.

You've likely had experiences where you made eye contact with someone you didn't know and you immediately looked away. It's an instinctual reaction based on fear. But fear of what exactly? They had the guts to look at you, so why not maintain eye contact until they are too uncomfortable to keep looking? In fact, when you maintain eye contact with many people they often can't help but smile. This is a simple way of training confidence as you endure very mild awkwardness and then realize you are completely safe.

Looking down or away can signal lower status or shame, as your confidence increases prolonged eye contact becomes easier.

Don't hunt with your eyes

When you enter a venue and hunt with your eyes for someone to approach it can look very needy. It reduces people to targets to be won over.

More importantly, it shows you aren't enjoying the moment, which is also unattractive.

You may actually have some very interesting people standing right next to you, but you will never know because you refused to talk to them. They weren't attractive enough for you for whatever reason.

While it's great to have standards, it doesn't mean you can't be friendly with everyone. This sort of behavior keeps you stuck in your head.

You are looking to the future for fulfilment instead of enjoying the present moment. It shows you aren't satisfied with what you have right now. So next time just see who is nearby and start talking. When you show you are satisfied with the reality you already have it is very attractive because it shows you don't *need* anything. So obviously when you are scanning the room for a target it shows you are suffering from a feeling of scarcity and need someone external to satisfy that need.

You don't need to worry about what is happening elsewhere in the room. Be happy with whatever you happen to be doing. Another benefit of appreciating the present moment is that people will be drawn to interact with you as you are providing positive emotions instead of trying to take them from others.

It's often easy to recognize what's going on inside someone by their body language in this way. The socially inexperienced don't realize how much of an open book they actually are to socially intelligent people. By working on your internal confidence and fixing poor body language you can make a much better impression and greatly improve your social interactions.

Here are some more bad habits to fix:

- Afraid to take up space
- Afraid to make any noise
- Hunched forward
- Crossed arms
- Holding a stiff position
- Playing with your phone to avoid interaction
- Speaking too quickly
- Speaking too quietly
- Moving too quickly
- Jerky hand movements
- Stuttering

- Hands in pocket
- Especially hands in pocket with thumbs sticking out
- Hands held in front of you
- Hands holding something in front of you
- Rubbing hands
- Scratching
- Verbal fillers (uh, um, so..like..)
- Always Repeating what people say
- Avoiding eye contact
- Upspeak
- Changing the subject to avoid talking about yourself
- Nervous laughter (When someone criticizes or calls you out on something for example.)

When you do these actions you can look nervous and shy.

Crossing your arms can mean you are nervous or don't trust someone so want to put up a barrier. Keep in mind it could also mean a person is just cold. Instead you can let your arms hang by your side. A similar sign is holding a drink in front of you. It's a subtle form of protection. Alternatively you could lower your hand to your side and hold the drink from the top. It looks more relaxed.

Hunching forward and similar body language increases the stress hormone cortisol. You will look submissive and feel nervous so try to avoid it. Good posture signals confidence and enhances attractiveness. There have been studies in which people guess who the leader of a group is. They often guessed the people with the best posture instead of the actual leaders.

To take advantage of this, keep your back straight, shoulders back, chest up, and observe this posture in the mirror. Check to make sure you are doing it well. Memorize this sensation and repeat it when you remember.

Taking up space is another obvious sign of confidence. When we feel uncomfortable we might try to hide as much of ourselves as possible. In extreme cases people might huddle in a corner with their hands over their head to protect themselves. Studies have shown that postures such as this increase cortisol and lower testosterone. Taking up space reduces cortisol and increases testosterone and other positive hormones.

It might occasionally be useful to hide from a threat. But in most social interactions the threat is only in the mind. Taking up more space than you need may seem unnecessarily selfish if you are used to constantly accommodating the needs and wants of others. But that desire to be a people pleaser is a symptom of fear. You might be scared people won't like you if you don't sacrifice your own space or comfort for them. There are definitely times to be selfless. It is still a virtue. However, when you sacrifice your own comfort for others keep in mind why you are doing it. When you do it because you want something from others, such as approval, it is really toxic and drains your energy.

Practice taking up more space. Stand with your feet wider. When you sit feel free to use the same relaxed posture you may use at home or when you are talking with friends. Below are more tips for fixing nervous body language.

Lean Back

When sitting with people you've just met leaning back may be more attractive than leaning forward. Depending on the situation of course. If someone says something you find extremely fascinating it's completely natural to lean in, tilt your head to the side a bit and ask follow up questions. The problem is when you lean in and give that attention only because you want someone's approval but in reality you weren't actually interested in what they were saying. You see this sort of approval seeking behavior in men and women towards each other. Usually the approval seeker thinks they are not good enough to keep the other's person's attention so they try to compliment or feign interest in even boring topics for fear of losing an opportunity.

By knowing when to lean back you show a bit of boredom and disengagement. Confident people are comfortable leaning back when nothing is genuinely attracting their attention. It's not necessarily a ploy to force people to entertain you, it's just a potential way of expressing something you might actually be feeling. Again, that is the point of this book, to help you express yourself honestly because that is true confidence and comfort in being yourself.

Mirroring

Mirroring is when people mimic the behaviors of others they interact with. You have likely been having a meal with a friend, took a drink and then your friend did the same or vice versa. Another common example is that people walking next to each other will often walk in sync with each other without even realizing it.

We are constantly influenced by what we see others doing. Here is an interesting example: An experiment had 2 groups watch different videos. One was about old people. And the other about athletes. The groups who watched the video about old people took longer to get out of their seat after watching how the elderly moved and they walked slower than people who watched the video about athletes. Other people are constantly influencing your behavior, even if you are only looking at recorded images of them.

Mirroring is an unconscious sign of rapport and connection. People who never mirror others are less likely to have friends. Mirroring is a natural part of building friendships. People are constantly mirroring body language, the words people use, humor style, foul language, talking speed, energy level, and other behaviors. Pay attention to this and occasionally use it intentionally.

Although mirroring is essential to socializing you shouldn't act incongruently from what you're comfortable with. Some people learn about mirroring and go overboard copying everything other people do. They become fixated with using mirroring as a technique and completely forget about building an actual connection with another person. Getting to know the other person is the goal. When you can relax and focus on the interaction mirroring should happen naturally. Mirroring only demonstrates you are beginning to trust each other so use it when appropriate.

Walk confidently

How do confident people walk?

They usually maintain good posture and look straight ahead into the direction they are moving.

They move with purpose and expect people to move out of their way. Because they expect it, people usually do get out of the way because they could otherwise be crushed.

People passing by can see the determination in your eyes if you don't intend deviate from the straight line you are walking. Though oddly sometimes people are socially retarded and oblivious to their environment. They inevitably crash into people twice their size or let their drink or phone get knocked out of their hand. It's an important lesson on paying attention to their surroundings and hopefully they've learned from their mistakes.

Power Pose

Stand with your feet a little more than shoulder width apart, and raise your hands above your head. Look up and smile. This pose has been shown to lower cortisol and increase testosterone and adrenaline.

Slow Down

Nervousness is often expressed in moving or speaking too fast. Some people worry they will be interrupted so try to say everything as quickly as possible.

Those lacking confidence may be worried others don't even care about what they have to add to the conversation so don't believe in the importance of what they are saying.

A confident leader believes his team will listen to everything he says. He can't imagine he would ever be interrupted. With this self-assurance he doesn't need to spit out his statements as quickly as possible. He can slow down. He can emphasize key words, he can speak a little slower than natural to get people focused on his story, or he could speed it back up if necessary. When you are confident and relaxed you are much more open to the infinite ways of expressing yourself.

Similarly, it can look more confident to slow down your movements. Your gestures will be smoother and more natural when done slowly and deliberately. For example, which looks better: Someone nearby says your name and immediately your head jerks like a rocket to the side and your eyes open wide at the surprise, or you slowly shift your gaze in that direction until you make eye contact with that person and give a smile?

Obviously the second choice. This is because in the second choice you had complete control of your actions. It wasn't an automatic response. It also shows you aren't just a simple animal reacting to the environment. It comes across as more relaxed and shows you haven't been bothered.

In any situation you can practice this too. Pay attention to when your body language becomes faster than necessary. It's often because of nervousness, or fear.

If you often jump at surprises, you might be too sensitive. Maybe something traumatic once scared you and now the slightest provocation triggers an overreaction. Such as a loud noise. In some situations, jumping or shouting may be appropriate. Train yourself to recognize when a situation is harmless.

Question inflection

Another voice related sign of fear is the tone of your voice. Confident people only use the raised inflection at the end of a question when they actually ask a question. However those lacking confidence who feel they have lower status often use the question inflection even when they make statements. For example, a confident person may hand you a glass of water and say, "This is *water*." When he gets to the last word it might even have a deeper inflection to emphasize the certainty in the statement. However, a shy person may hand you the water and say, "This is *water*?" It will sound similar to a question even though it isn't.

The subtexts of those two scenarios are completely different. The confident person is sharing an absolute statement. He knows it's water and is just letting you know. The shy person isn't actually asking a question, but the raised tone implies he is seeking rapport and is worried about the other person's opinion. The confident person's tone is more authoritative. Whereas the shy person's rising tone can seem weak or untrustworthy.

The way you speak conveys who you are and what you are feeling. It conveys if you think you are a loser or not. When you think you don't belong your voice and body language will let people know. If you don't believe you are worthy of their friendship then why should they?

Question inflection when you don't need it is an example of thinking you are a loser. Speaking with confidence can help you hold people's attention no matter what you are actually talking about.

Speak loud and clear enough so people can hear you easily. I know that sounds like great advice for someone who already has a bit of confidence.

When you are shy sometimes you open your mouth but the words either won't come out or they come out in a jumbled mess. You might think it's pathetic. But it's healthier to find humor in it. Laugh it off as a brain fart and show you don't let those moments hurt your feelings.

The only truly pathetic thing would be to give up just because you've had a few awkward conversations. It will take some practice but eventually you will be speaking with more authority in your voice.

Find the lowest natural pitch of your speaking voice as this is more confident and attractive. It's mesmerizing and people can't help but listen.

A clear, slow, deep voice can have a tremendous impact on your social interactions as well as your emotional state.

Training

To improve body language you must start paying attention to it. Spend a week or more focusing on how you present yourself to the world and make adjustments as necessary. Pay attention to how you speak and move in social situations such as parties. Also pay attention to how you interact with all people, such as cashiers and bus drivers.

Whenever your body language or voice exposes your fears take note of what triggered it. Later you can write it down in your journal and reflect on why that event made it difficult to express yourself. This will help you eliminate bad habits. It will however take courage to be honest with yourself.

Pay attention to even small things such as fidgeting, scratching, adjusting your hair, *(who are you trying to impress?),* slouching, avoiding eye contact, or stepping out of someone's way. These habits may all indicate submissiveness, fear and lack of confidence.

Analyze yourself and question your behavior. If you dare, go deep with your questions.

Ask yourself:

- Why did I react that way?
- Do I always do that?
- When was the last time I reacted that way?
- When did I start reacting that way?
- Is this just a habit?
- How do I feel in those situations?
- Why do I feel like this?
- Do I need to improve my behavior?
- How will I improve?
- What will I do next time?

Spend at least a week observing yourself and making an effort to improve your body language. You will see some improvements. Eventually as you work on inner confidence expressing it in your words and actions will become more natural and won't take a conscious effort. In this first week it might take a lot of energy to observe and adjust your bad habits, however it is very much worth it as the new habits will become who you are.

Chapter 3: How to Quickly Get Into a Social Mood without Alcohol

"I think the warning labels on alcoholic beverages are too bland. They should be more vivid. Here is one I would suggest: "Alcohol will turn you into the same asshole your father was."
— **George Carlin**

Alcohol is known as a social lubricant. It's associated with loss of inhibitions, confusion, poor decision-making and a long list of damaging side effects to the brain and body that you learned in your high school health class but quickly forgot after your first sip.

People love alcohol because it neutralizes the parts of the brain responsible for making decisions. This makes it easier to talk to people. That's what people really want. To be able to forget about nonsensical worries and self-doubt to build connections with others. Alcohol is just a crutch people abuse to get there. But as you already know, this tasty poison can be deadly. The Center for Disease Control reports that each year between 2006 and 2010 more than 88,000 Americans died from excessive alcohol consumption. In 2014 at least 9,967 Americans died in alcohol impaired driving crashes.

You've likely stumbled across similar statistics before. Maybe you didn't even care. Maybe you thought, "Those poor bastards." But if you are a drinker it never changed your behavior. After all, you are a responsible adult. You can choose to put whatever you want into your body and live with the consequences. A drink or two once in a while is entirely reasonable. Moderation is the key. In fact doctors suggest a glass of alcohol once in a while has some health benefits. However the problem is that people often rely on alcohol to be themselves. Alcohol becomes a crutch. You'll never learn to walk if you keep holding on to it.

"It's a great advantage not to drink among hard drinking people."
— **F. Scott Fitzgerald**, **The Great Gatsby**

There are alternatives to alcohol for confident interaction with people you've just met in a venue where alcohol consumption is expected.

The strategy:

1. **Keep talking to new people**
2. **Minimize time between interactions**
3. **Don't let uncomfortable experiences prevent more interactions**
4. **Stay present to the moment**

When you enter a social venue and you start a conversation with someone new enjoy the interaction and see where it leads. Don't depend on this one new friend to feel valuable.

Feel free to go meet more people.

Often people latch on to a friend in social interactions and are scared to meet new people. The moment are alone is scary because you might not make any new friends. You might have a great chat with a new acquaintance but what will happen when this new acquaintance leaves?

You may feel a confidence boost when you first meet someone. But if that new person leaves the venue how would you feel? Depending on the severity of your social anxiety your emotions might plummet back to negativity as you doubt your ability to start another conversation.

A shy guy will be nervous to talk to a woman, (attractive or otherwise). He doesn't usually start conversations with new people, but he is determined to develop his confidence by facing his irrational fears. After she gave a friendly reaction he relaxed and was able to ask some questions he actually found interesting.

They had a great conversation for about 7 minutes. The time really flew by because he was enjoying the moment. He was able to forget about a majority of his insecurities. But then she left to meet her friends somewhere else.

He was alone again. And suddenly those doubts and insecurities returned. They will always be there if you never resolve them. Later we will discuss effective methods to do this. For now just remember to minimize the time between interactions, especially when you go out alone.

The more you hesitate to socialize when part of you actually wants to take action, the more energy you will lose. You will feel more tired and negative. Your mind will flood with thoughts like: *"I want to talk to her, but she's walking too fast. I want to meet those guys but I don't think I'm cool enough. I should say hi to that guy... ok getting closer, oh no I can't do it he's busy."*

You can likely relate to this scenario in which part of you wants to meet people however you feel the fear inside you. It often manifests as a heavy sensation in the chest. As a result, you make up a random excuse as to why you shouldn't take action. This is like driving a car and constantly hitting the gas to go but then suddenly hitting the brakes.

Doing this over and over isn't good for the car and just wastes fuel. In the same way this behavior depletes your energy. You are focusing on a goal: meeting new people and developing confidence. You have opportunities in front of you but lack of experience leads to fear, which leads to excuses and inaction.

Investing in inaction makes you feel more and more like a loser incapable of meeting new people.

If however you invest in action and talk to many people and engage with them positively it changes your brain chemistry to that of a person who can fearlessly engage others.

Your brain will provide the neurotransmitters and hormones to make you feel like whatever kind of person you believe you are. The belief comes first. You have to earn the right to believe you are confident. Otherwise your brain will continue to produce the chemistry of a person troubled with self-doubt or any other insecurity you've allowed into your mind.

Eventually you adapt to this process and it becomes easier to start conversations with anyone. You will gradually build the framework of a confident mind through experience. This is why it's essential to not react to people who don't engage with you. Maybe the other person is in a bad mood. On a different day they would have been happy to talk with you. You don't know what is going on in people's lives or what nonsense they are dealing with. It really doesn't matter anyway because there are plenty of other options. Go meet some other people who will actually appreciate you.

You don't need to lie to yourself that what you perceive as rejection can hurt. Some people can be incredibly rude. It's often just a manifestation of their insecurities. Though there are other possibilities. But this doesn't mean you need to shut down your emotions and hide under a bulletproof shell of shame. You can keep talking to more people. Eventually you will meet someone who will be happy to meet you.

When you are social with new people it has an intense impact on your emotional state because it's based on your beliefs about yourself.

If you never feel safe it shuts down your ability to express yourself.

If everyone was constantly rejecting you this emotional torture would make you want to hide your real self from others.

People might not even be rejecting you, but that fear of rejection stems from your own feelings of inadequacy. If you think you aren't good enough, that is how you will feel.

The emotions you feel in any situation trigger your behavior. When you aren't feeling safe you naturally want to hide yourself.

Luckily the opposite is of course also true. When you are getting good reactions you interpret it as evidence that people appreciate and approve of you. This belief leads to positive emotions. You no longer feel the need to hide. You can come out from behind that protective shell you formed when you felt unlovable. Talking with anyone becomes effortless and you don't even need alcohol to do it.

After fun interactions all day or night you might go home and not be able to sleep because of how energized you feel. Conversely if you are in a negative, hateful state of mind and you think people are only talking to the most attractive ones in the room and intentionally ignoring you then every failed attempt to start an interaction will sting a little more. Every refusal of your attention will be seen as an intentional rejection. It will hurt and you'll go home exhausted as you spent your energy on trying to win over the validation of others to prove your own self-worth.

For now, realize that it is useful to stay present to the moment and talk to as many people as possible. You don't need to hunt for the most interesting people in the room. You can find something interesting about every person you meet.

This process pumps your state.

The more people you talk to the more positive you will feel.

The more energy will flow through you as your body releases the hormones of happiness, such as dopamine and serotonin.

You don't need to first memorize an encyclopedia of social skills. You just need to take action. This is something anyone can experience if they try. Even socially anxious people will tell you stories of how they let loose and suddenly have a fun night when they get a bit drunk. Their inhibitions were finally released and they could be themselves with a bit of mental impairment. But even better results are available while sober if you can force yourself to interact with many people in a short amount of time. You can experience this for yourself. Here is how:

1. Choose a day you have free time
2. Find a social event you'd like to attend
3. If you can't find an event then go to a social venue in the evening such as a bar or club
4. Practice the concepts we've discussed up to this point

This concept is incredibly effective. It not only does not require alcohol to get you socializing but it can bring some amazing new experiences into your life. You will start to feel more confident. There is however a small catch I should be honest with you about. When you are constantly socializing like this in the moment you will feel amazing. However, if you take a break from it for a period of time your doubts and insecurities may return.

You may feel confused. After all, you've been having more success. People have shown they like you. You thought you had confidence figured out and you could pull it out anytime you want.

There are two reasons for this.

First, every habit you build is always in your brain. However, the more you engage in a habit the stronger that connection becomes and the more likely it will be repeated.

The less you engage in a habit the less likely it is to return thought it still could. If you have shy socially avoidant habits they won't be instantly erased by a few days of confident interaction. You need to practice the confident habits daily for them to strengthen and become your natural behavior.

There is also an even more important reason for the relapse back to your socially anxious habits. Though you've broken the code of how to feel confident temporarily, you still haven't resolved the internal issues that prevent you from feeling happy about being yourself. Do this confidence is a natural result.

Chapter 4: Real Happiness

"Realize that true happiness lies within you. Waste no time and effort searching for peace and contentment and joy in the world outside. Remember that there is no happiness in having or in getting, but only in giving. Reach out. Share. Smile. Hug. Happiness is a perfume you cannot pour on others without getting a few drops on yourself."
— **Og Mandino**

Social media and the self-help industry are infested with quotes and advice on attaining happiness. It can sound positive on the surface, such as these prolific statements:

"Money can't buy us happiness. But it can pay for the internet. Which is the same thing."

"The secret to happiness is to have a bad memory."

"Never put the key to your happiness in someone else's pocket."

These statements may sound inspiring. However when you buy into them it only serves to reinforce the belief that you lack happiness and need to chase it. They condition you to run away from your negative emotions in pursuit of something that feels better.

The desire for happiness is in fact very negative because it only makes you feel worse about not being in a good mood. It only reinforces a sense of lack. Accepting negative experiences and emotions is actually the most positive thing you can do.

Philosopher Alan Watts called this the Law of Reverse Effort or the Backwards Law to illustrate how making an effort inevitably causes problems. He wrote, *"When you try to stay on the surface of the water, you sink; but when you try to sink, you float. Insecurity is the result of trying to find safety ... Contrary to common sense, saving and mental health are the result of radical faith that we have no chance to save ourselves."*

The more you chase happiness the less happy you will be. You will also require more external validation to occasionally get a glimpse of positive emotions.

For example, assuming you are a shy guy, maybe you feel happy when a girl smiles at you. Finally you feel worthy of female attention. But the high you got from a smile soon wears off. Soon you need to constantly tell jokes to get good reactions from women because your self-esteem depends on that positive attention.

When you are externally validated you will require more and more of this positive female attention to maintain your good mood. If you suddenly abstain from socializing for a few weeks it could hit your emotions as hard as an addicted smoker who tries to quit cold turkey after smoking a pack or more a day for years.

The more desperate you are for love and attention the lonelier you will feel.

The more you envy good looking people the uglier you will feel.

The more you envy confident people the more insecure and socially awkward you will feel.

When you envy the social skills and self-esteem of the confident guy you are only convincing yourself that you lack those traits. If you start training yourself to "be confident," You are only reinforcing the belief that you lack confidence. Social confidence shouldn't be your goal because it would mean you believe you don't have it and need to chase it. If you keep chasing this goal it will always remain out of reach. Start looking inside yourself and you will see the barriers to the confidence that already resides within you.

An important variable is wanting versus needing. If you only want something, you can accept not receiving it. If you feel you need it, you think you will die without it. The only things you really need are water, air, food, and arguably, human interaction. The risk of not attaining anything else doesn't need to impact your emotions as much as you let it.

In fact, when you let go of needing something you are much more likely to achieve it. I play billiards and I notice that it's often easier to sink more balls in the beginning of a game because I'm just enjoying the moment. However towards the end of a game when I only need to sink the last ball to win it can take forever because I care so much about winning. Caring about something too much gets you stuck in your own head worrying about the future.

You worry about if you will get it or not and it messes you up. If you could let go of the need for perfection you would relax more, making it easier to achieve your goal.

To let go it's necessary to honestly confront your pain and fear to develop courage. Paradoxically, avoiding pain is more painful than accepting it.

Pain is growth.

As some say, "pain is weakness leaving the body."

If you live your life running away from pain and insecurity then you will never be happy. Without authentic, internally validated happiness it will be difficult to ever really feel confident.

When you are happy it is easy to enjoy the moment.

Your concerns for the future don't weigh on you.

Memories of failure don't haunt you.

You are released from these fears and confidence becomes inevitable.

When this happens it may seem that you instantly learned charisma and memorized an encyclopedia of social skills. However, you have only reconnected with your original state. You have found happiness within yourself. This happiness is an indication of your own satisfaction with life and reality. If you are content then it is only natural that you express yourself confidently.

Many young children sing, dance, and jump around acting silly in public. They aren't afraid of expressing themselves. You rarely see adults doing this. Adults usually need the excuse of alcohol to act like that. Social pressure usually prevents such freedom and connection to natural happiness. As we grow up the pressure to gain social acceptance increases. Happiness is still there, it's just been hidden by many layers of social conditioning.

This is exactly what many people suffering from severe social anxiety and depression experience when they first start taking antidepressants.

Some say this medicine gives a break from relentless darkness. Some say it's like they've been living in a dark room and then suddenly someone turns on the light. Of course not everyone is helped by medication but it often does reset the brain's chemistry in a way that minimizes oppressive negativity.

If your issues are severe it may be helpful to try medication. However they can only resolve the symptoms of your troubles at best. At least make a serious effort to improve yourself on your own first or find a Cognitive Behavioral Therapist.

Many people in online depression and anxiety communities seem to have already given up on taking responsibility for their own emotions.

People trying to get off medication gradually, even with the help of a doctor are often ridiculed by those who've convinced themselves they can't function without their own meds.

Methods of coping with stress and facing emotional problems honestly are often dismissed. Of course this doesn't describe everyone in these communities. I just happen to have observed many people leaving comments complaining about their life, seeking attention and justifying their addictions. They claim to have no control over their actions and emotions. But in reality they don't seem to want control.

If it was offered to them they wouldn't take it because they are obsessed with their victim mentality. They feel victimized by their brain chemistry, other people or even the weather. Playing the victim is an excuse to give up on life, happiness, and responsibility for one's own actions.

What's worse is it will often be impossible to convince people of this. After all, they already feel terrible and they just can't dig themselves out of those emotions.

With the victim mentality they feel sorry for themselves, feel attacked by the world or their body. They become stuck in sadness and self-pity. People engage in these behaviors for attention and validation.

They feel like failures.

They feel they can't get validation for anything they do.

As a result they feel the only way to ensure attention and recognition is by making people concerned with their plight. This gives them good feelings as others seem to care and try to help. However, the best advice is usually ignored because these 'victims' never wanted to resolve their issues. They only wanted attention.

When you feel like a victim you've also decided to avoid taking risks that could lead to rejection and failure. This leads to statements like:

"I shouldn't go to that party. I'm ugly no one would talk to me anyway."

"Nobody will ever love me. I don't need to ask anyone for a date."

Observe how convenient that is. They've already decided their future. The negative thoughts are just excuses to avoid expressing their real self. They still want to hide behind that protective shell. They can avoid responsibility for any difficult decision.

They can feel like they understand the world: *"Girls only date good looking rich guys. So a loser like me will always be alone."*-read in an annoying high pitch voice.

They don't need to look for evidence to the contrary because they don't need it.

They've already decided what the world looks like.

They know everything.

They are experts on reality and within this reality there is no need to make an effort to change.

They are happy to believe they've got it all figured out. Even though that warped illogical understanding is based on nothing but avoiding confrontation with reality.

These benefits can become addictive. People often become addicted to whatever emotional state they often find themselves in. This is easily observable in most people. Some people are constantly angry and complaining, others are usually more positive and outgoing. The victim mentality can be treated. It takes some effort to acknowledge when you wish people would pay more attention to your efforts. Being honest with yourself is an essential part of the methods presented in this book. You may not have a severe case of playing the victim but be honest with yourself and you might realize some immature moments of begging for pity.

How to Overcome Victim Mentality

1. Don't be the victim

To get out of the victim mentality you will need to give up the warped benefits we just discussed. You will need to take responsibility for your actions. You need to accept that everything that happens to you is the consequence of your own actions.

Some people might belittle you and prevent you from opportunities. But your biggest victimizer is likely yourself! There are obviously exceptions as some people have gone through some truly horrific trauma. However, the truth remains that most people are their own greatest victimizers.

A kid in school may have called you names. You may have been scolded by your boss. A group of people may have even ganged up to prevent you from achieving one of your goals. But those people will only have as large an impact on your life as you allow.

When you've made poor decisions, wasted time, avoided opportunities, and given up on your responsibility to develop yourself you continuously victimized yourself in ways other people are incapable of forcing upon you.

There is no point claiming to be a poor emotional victim when you've treated yourself much worse. You may have wasted hours and weeks of your life thinking about how the world has wronged you. Those negative thoughts don't help you. They just waste your time and energy. It's just another example of how you are victimizing yourself.

Instead of complaining about how the world treats you start looking for opportunities to improve your situation.

Instead of complaining about how badly your friends treat you start looking for new friends!

Instead of complaining about how your girlfriend doesn't respect you go find a new girlfriend.

Focus on what you can control. Such as your emotional reactions. The choices you make lead to the life you live.

2. Take responsibility for your life

Having control over your life and decisions is a major determinant of happiness and success.

In one study groups of young students were asked to work on math puzzles. When the students received the results, one group was told, "You did well, you must have worked hard," And the other group was told "You did well, you must be very smart." The students were then asked to work on one more set of puzzles. The students who were told they must have worked hard performed the best. And most importantly, they enjoyed the puzzles much more than the second group. The group which was told they must be very smart first worked on the easy puzzles first. They were intent on proving they were smart. If they couldn't finish the difficult puzzles it might imply they aren't smart. They felt more pressure to prove this which may be why they didn't enjoy the activity as much as their peers.

The first group who was told they must have worked hard only needed to demonstrate their ability to work hard. Most of these students also attempted the difficult puzzles first. It's something that is within anyone's control. Whereas smartness is seen as natural and out of our control. In much the same way, whenever something is in your control it makes life more enjoyable.

Believing you have no control over circumstances in your life hurts your self-esteem. Blaming others and external factors instead of admitting your role in mistakes you've made only empowers a toxic victim mentality.

When you fail it's healthy to admit what you can do better next time. You might make the same mistake again because you are only human and that's ok. The important thing is to take responsibility for your life. When you do this it's also easier to minimize reliance on external validation. You are less likely to need people constantly praising you to feel good about yourself.

People with the victim mentality are also often accused of being "attention whores." This need for attention comes from feeling insecure. They need people to praise them, especially for superficial things like their looks in order to feel loved and appreciated. This sickness can be alleviated by taking responsibility for their own happiness. When this happens compliments won't be as necessary because they will start developing their own internal validation. When you have emotional stability you won't need to waste as much time on worrying what other people think about you.

3. Be grateful for what you have

No matter how bad your life may be there is always someone who has it much worse. Whenever you want to play the victim role just ask yourself,

"Do other people in the world have it worse than me?"

The answer will most likely be yes. If you are reading this book you are likely from a country where you have a lot more opportunity than most people in the world.

Can you imagine if you had been born 200 years ago? Life was so much more arduous and painful back then. The opportunities available now did not exist. How many things do you possess and experience that people a century ago would have seen as magic? Cell phones, computers, cars, video games, knowledge of our reality and more. People didn't have these back then. Average people in developed countries live better than kings did centuries ago and yet there is no appreciation for this fact. People are never satisfied.

It's amazing, for example, how people can complain about flights. You are flying thousands of miles in the sky. You are flying! It would have been seen as magic a few centuries ago, and passengers still complain about annoying little things such as no snacks or bad service and then let these complaints ruin their entire day. They could be flying to a tropical paradise for a few days but will inevitably find something to complain about.

When you are feeling bad take a moment to be grateful for what you do have in life. It changes your perspective from being angry at what you lack to being appreciative of what you have.

You likely have a lot more than you realize. Everything happens in your life is given to you for a reason. It's an opportunity to learn and grow. If life throws a disappointment at you the best choice you can make is to ask yourself:

"Where is the opportunity in this?"

For example. You might get fired from your job. Initially you'll be worried about finding your next job, not having enough money to eat, and similar concerns.

You could shut down in a spiral of negativity and give up on being a part of society, or you could look for opportunities and see what is actually available to you. You could start your own online freelancing business, or find a better job you like even more. Focusing on the solution is much more productive. It also supports positive emotions.

When you feel discouraged and disappointed it is encouragement to change your situation. Focus on opportunities and you will find them. There have been studies indicating that optimistic people are luckier. They are more open to the opportunities available to them. Whereas pessimistic people could walk by a 100 dollar bill on the road and not even see it. You usually only see what you are willing to look for.

4. Forgive

Holding a grudge is like drinking poison and expecting the other person to die. Thinking angry thoughts and plotting revenge is only killing you. It weakens your heart, stresses you out and shortens your life.

Forgiving someone is not for them to relax in the knowledge you won't be pursuing a vicious revenge. It is for you to move on with your life. When you focus on the wrongs done to you your mind is stuck in the past. It prevents you from progressing. If someone hurt you, those thoughts of how much you hate them will occasionally resurface. You still haven't let go of the pain they caused you. Don't get trapped in the past. Learn to let go. Forgiveness dissolves the emotional link to the people who hurt you. If a thought of how they wronged you resurfaces there will no longer be a need to attach a painful emotion to it. You will have freed yourself from that negativity.

5. Help people

The victim mentality is very low energy. As a result these so called 'victims' try to take energy and value from others. They are focused on what others can do for them. Such as provide pity, attention and support.

To reverse this, simply ask yourself how you can provide value to others.

This shifts focus from how other people can satisfy you to how you can make other people a little happier. Look for opportunities to help people. Maybe you have some advice that could help them out. If you look for opportunities to provide you will definitely find something. Doing some volunteer work will of course also be very humbling.

Hopefully you aren't engaging in much victim mentality behavior at this point. You are however now prepared for when those types of thoughts arise. Playing the victim role prevents the genuine self-expression required for real happiness.

You are capable of taking responsibility for your own life and decisions. With that responsibility you can reconnect with your happiness and express yourself confidently.

The victim mentality is a massive limiting belief. Confidence is the ability to express yourself without limiting beliefs or concerns of what others think of you. So if you want confidence you will have to eliminate any traces of playing the victim. You will also have to retrain a few other bad habits you've picked up.

Confidence is only your natural state. As babies humans are only naturally afraid of 2 things. Loud noises and falling from high places. Every other fear is learned. The fear of strangers. The fear of people laughing at you. The fear of making mistakes. These are all learned habits than can similarly be unlearned. At least you can train yourself to react more appropriately to situations that usually triggered your fear response.

Fear blocks the ability to feel happy. Imagine if you could control the ability to feel happy any time. In theory this is possible, but it takes a lot of training and self-discipline. For most people fearful responses are learned and constantly reinforced as they encounter similar situations over and over again. Even though they try to react more positively, it takes effort and practice to relax in some situations. The brain has evolved to behave this way for good reason. If you could easily maintain a happy state at all times your addiction to it would prevent you from taking appropriate action in dangerous situations. A tiger may approach you and you wouldn't even consider running. Even as you were about to be devoured you would still feel ecstatic. The negative emotions are there to give you impetus to change something. They are speaking to you and you only need to listen instead of running away from them.

Facing pain allows you to be honest with yourself. Being honest with yourself allows you to dissolve the walls you've put up to protect yourself from scrutiny for fear of ridicule and rejection. Given time and commitment you can reconnect with your original happiness. This will allow you to express yourself confidently as you won't be as concerned with meeting everyone's standards.

Real happiness comes from within. You may have heard that concept before. It's not just a cliché. You have within you the potential for states of ecstatic joy you would not believe existed without first experiencing them. The potential is within you already. You don't need to take mind altering chemicals to do it either.

There is of course also the temporary spike in emotions when you get something you want. You might feel good but that emotional reaction will fade. This keeps you chasing more and more of those enjoyable moments as you run away from self-doubt.

If you have a lot to work on such as financial security, your appearance, health, relationships, fixing bad habits, overweight and so on it's easy to look to the future for happiness. You can convince yourself that when those issues are resolved you can finally be happy.

You pretend it's only those external issues that need to be fixed and then life will be perfect. However, plenty of wealthy successful individuals will tell you money and fame never made them happy. It obviously can improve your life and buy you a higher class of memories, but financial stability will never buy you happiness. Some people achieve everything they could ever want but still feel that emptiness inside pulling them towards more and more stimulation to avoid looking within for happiness.

We all have pain and stress locked within us. It weighs down on the carefree confident version of ourselves holding onto it. To ignore how uncomfortable it feels to be alone with these feelings people are addicted to distractions. If you are outside and have an hour to sit and wait for your friends what's the first thing you will do? For many people they will find something to play with on their phone. Some people stay home all day playing video games and watching movies alone. Countless hours spent on distraction and hardly a moment spent on introspection.

We all have emotional memories we've never resolved. We all have parts of ourselves we've hidden in order to gain acceptance in society. Maybe as a child you were talking in the car and your father demanded you shut up. It didn't matter that your father wanted to focus on the road for a moment. To you it was a traumatic experience. You didn't just hear the words "shut up." You interpreted it as "shut up or I'll throw you out of the car and abandon you." As a child you are terrified of losing the love of your parents because you depend on them for your survival. You do whatever they say even if it means suppressing your desire to express yourself because you feel your entire existence depends on it.

Part of you wanted to be talkative and humorous. But when your father told you to "shut up," you hid that part of yourself and pretended it wasn't there.

You became ashamed of it and started to hate it to the point you hated its presence in anyone.

But it is still there, hidden by the pressure you felt to avoid expressing it. Whenever you feel like being talkative it will trigger that same resistance you felt as a child. Each time you resist the behavior will also grow stronger.

In the future you may even feel compelled to shame other people for similar behavior. Someone may be talking loudly and you scream at them to shut it. It is more motivated by the desire to reinforce your own identity as a person who does the socially acceptable thing rather than to change people's behavior.

To combat this you can start by forcing yourself to be more talkative. It will be difficult at first but it will reinforce new habits that negate the old ones. You will feel the tug of resistance as you try to engage in behavior you were once discouraged from. This is natural but that feeling doesn't need to control your life anymore.

There is of course more to the process of resolving those internal issues that prevent real happiness and subsequently get in the way of your confidence.

Distractions such as TV, phone games, social media and so on give you a boost of positive neurotransmitters. This is easily confused for a form of "happiness," but the feeling soon fades and you need to continue engaging in that distraction to maintain the feeling. You feel good after watching an episode of your favorite show and feel compelled to watch another episode even though you have already stayed awake 2 hours past your usual sleeping time.

These distractions not only feel good in the moment but they also provide relief from critical self-analysis and other negative thoughts that might emerge if you were to sit alone with yourself and quietly think.

Without the distractions you might be forced to confront the fact your base emotional state is very negative and infested with fears.

It's as if you are usually 3 out of 10 on a scale of happiness, but the distractions increase that score temporarily. Whenever you take a break from distractions you snap back to a miserable 3 out of 10.

This can also apply to working on improving external elements of your life. Such as health, money, career, developing skills, achieving goals and other areas you would consider very positive. Of course these areas should be worked on, but if you haven't worked on real inner confidence first it can feel like a juggling act as you are constantly pulled back to feeling like a failure even after you've experienced some success.

Maybe you've made progress learning some social skills and even practicing what you've learned for a few days. But that success isn't lasting.

Deep down you still don't believe you are good enough for people to talk to you. You still haven't resolved this fear and the feelings of inferiority still limit your behavior.

When you work on accepting and understanding yourself you can begin to resolve a lot of these issues preventing real progress.

The negativity and fear will keep pulling you back because it's something you need to be constantly reminded of.

When you ignore it these emotions can only get worse.

Often, the worse it feels the more you want to ignore it.

But that is counterproductive.

They are like giant anchors dragging on the bottom of the ocean. Ignoring them won't help your progress.

You need to pull them up and handle them with care to sail faster.

When you can accept these parts of yourself it's astonishing how much faster you can reach goals in other areas of your life.

Because this is what is required to really transform yourself.

Self-Acceptance: The key to real happiness

Everything about yourself you've perceived as inferior or unacceptable becomes suppressed. As social beings it's natural to be influenced by others. When you are exposed to norms that discourage certain beliefs and behaviors its natural you follow local rules to maintain acceptance within your community.

This is great for society. Individuals can be extremely selfish, greedy, and inconsiderate of the consequences of their actions to the point of causing extreme pain and chaos. Social pressure limits the ego's ability to do whatever it wants. However, this process of social pressure and shaming causes individuals to hide parts of themselves that are deemed unacceptable by others. Anything incompatible with the image we want to present to the world is suppressed.

To maintain acceptance by society everything you've been told to hate about yourself is disowned. This disowned self represents parts of us we refuse to accept. It contains both positive and negative qualities we've rejected in ourselves.

We all have the potential for selfishness, anger, sadness, love, humor, and generosity. When we are children the potential for expressing nearly every emotion and behavior is there. As we grow up we associate certain traits with being either acceptable or unacceptable.

We naturally have instinctual needs for safety, food, and belonging. If our parents inform us our behavior is unacceptable we may feel one of these needs is being threatened.

Maybe a child grows up in a family where they aren't allowed express themselves. When they try to do something creative like sing or paint pictures they are ridiculed. Or maybe they want to say silly things and act playfully but their parents scold them with reminders that they shouldn't have anything to be happy about. Teachers may scold students who show too much confidence and individuality. Classmates may ridicule a young boy who shows interest in a girl. In reaction he grows up scared to express his feelings to women.

These types of events threaten your instinctual needs. Approval of classmates, teachers, and especially parents is necessary for most young people to feel a sense of belonging. When ridiculed or scolded we adjust our behavior because it is necessary for survival.

Ignoring the disowned self is irresponsible. Ignored, these undesirable traits and impulses can sabotage relationships and prevent growth. Whatever traits we deny in ourselves we see in others. Psychology calls this projection. We project onto and condemn qualities in others we've tried to hide within us.

If you are annoyed at loud people there's a good chance you've suppressed your own loudness for example. These projections happen subconsciously. This mechanism allows people to view themselves as perfect and innocent. How we view ourselves can often be very different from the reality.

Projecting negative qualities onto others becomes an excuse to avoid fixing those traits within ourselves. It's always other people who are selfish, rude, inconsiderate, greedy, incompetent, lazy, angry, messy, intolerant, and so on.

They are the flawed human beings whereas we are perfect. We are satisfied with criticizing them instead of looking in the mirror and recognizing the same traits within ourselves.

But you can never be whole if you try to cut off parts of yourself that you may someday need in the future.

For example, Tim is a very nice guy. He's always smiling and friendly with everyone. He's always helpful to most people. He thinks offering unsolicited help to others will make them like him.

He is scared of confrontation. As a child bullies picked on him for various reasons. Once he hit a bully in the face to defend himself. His teacher scolded him and he was punished with a week of detention. Every time he would get upset his parents would respond with more anger and demand he shut up and stop whining. Sometimes they hit him. This made him afraid to express his own anger and discontent. When he grew up never reacted angrily to things that upset him.

On the plus side, this may be good for society. He isn't yelling and causing a scene over missing a flight because of a 'random' security check that wastes his time. But for Tim, this constant suppression of every instance of anger just builds up inside him. A girl agreed to a date with him then she flakes and doesn't show up. All his friends forget his birthday. Somebody bumps into him in the street and doesn't apologize. Other people within his company receives raises and he doesn't even though he worked harder than anyone. All the anger from these events doesn't disappear. It builds up until is someday explodes. If it doesn't explode it still festers and prevents real growth. Without integrating these disowned parts we aren't adequately prepared for all the nonsense life throws at us.

One day Tim is attacked by another man. Tim freezes. He has his back to the wall. He just wants to run away because as a people pleaser that is his usual response to confrontation. Part of him knows he should stand up for himself but he is too scared to try. If he could get in touch with his anger he could yell back at his attacker and intimidate him. But when he opens his mouth to shout nothing will come out. If needed he could strike back and the attacker would run away in search of an easier target. Instead the attacker sees Tim's weakness and inability to fight back as permission to continue tormenting him.

Even the negative aspects of ourselves we deny can be useful in appropriate situations. If you accept the angry part of yourself it doesn't mean you have to be an evil bully. The same with being selfish.

Overindulgent selfishness is destructive. Killing, stealing, hoarding resources, disrespecting people and destroying property without any concern for the consequences is not only detrimental to society but can quickly earn you many enemies. Having zero concern for yourself would be equally hazardous.

Your love of humanity might compel you to give away all your money and possessions. But this sacrifice could lead to you starving to death and taken advantage of by more selfish individuals. The key is obviously to find balance between your selfish desires and the compulsion to contribute to others. Find balance between expressing anger appropriately, and genuinely not letting people bother you. Find balance between the desires to be alone and among friends.

Ignoring your flaws will only make you compensate too far in the opposite direction. To remedy this it's time to take a serious look at what you might be compensating for.

It might not be comfortable but examining the disowned self provides immense opportunities for transformation.

Here are a few more crucial ways self-acceptance can improve your life:

1. Better relationships

As you integrate these previously disowned parts of yourself you become more complete. When you accept the more negative parts of yourself it's easier to accept them in others. As a result these behaviors in other people won't bother you as much as before.

You won't have as many negative thoughts preventing you from communicating effectively. Accepting yourself makes it easier for others to accept you too. It can lead to improved relationships at work, with friends, family and everyone you interact with.

People with too many disowned parts often give off a toxic needy vibe that impedes real communication and connection with other people.

This can come in the form of men approaching women they haven't met before and asking, "Excuse me miss, can we be friends?" Which I have observed before and it's as cringe worthy as it sounds. Especially since the subtext is, "I have no standards for who can be my friend, please be my friend! And by friend I mean more than friends but I'm not brave enough to admit that I'm interested in you as a man interested in a woman so I'll just pretend I only want friendship."

This sort of behavior can also be a sign a man has been shamed into suppressing his heterosexuality. There is nothing shameful about natural biological instincts.

These extremely suppressed individuals are often angry at the world and resent the rejection they feel they have suffered. In reality they first rejected themselves.

They need validation and praise from others to feel a sense of acceptance. When they don't receive it their condition only worsens.

By accepting yourself you avoid suffering in this way and relationships will likely improve.

2. More accurate view of the world

The more parts of yourself you have disowned the more distorted your worldview may become. This is because you need to continuously make up stories to justify your feelings and behavior.

When you accept yourself you no longer need to look at the world through the lens of denial. When you integrate these parts you accept your authentic self and don't need to hide who you really are anymore. You will have a clearer perception of who you are and your place in the world.

You can accurately examine the world around you. You'll be able to see many of your own destructive behaviors in others and understand their motivations. You won't need to lie to yourself as much anymore and this will open you up to truths about life.

If you assume everyone is judging you, scheming to take advantage of you and is not at all concerned for your wellbeing it can feel as if you've seriously evolved when you realize everyone is just doing the best they can and are dealing with their own suppressed emotions and many more problems. This new perspective helps you develop compassion.

3. More Energy

When you carry all this negative energy with you it stresses you out. This stress drains your energy. Every time a suppressed emotion reemerges to be dealt with it is shoved backed down even deeper. Such as an embarrassing memory that occasionally creeps back into your mind. Everyone involved has already forgotten that experience and moved on. But suddenly you think about it and feel stressed out about it.

One embarrassing memory may not seem too draining. But there is much more beneath the surface. Rejections, failures, scoldings, and other uncomfortable experiences are bundled together and dragged behind us everywhere we go. If you feel rejected all the unresolved emotions from previous rejections will come back to sting you. An emotionally healthy person wouldn't let it bother them. If someone doesn't want to talk they wouldn't take it personally and don't even see it as rejection. But the person with mountains of unresolved issues experiences one rejection and it's like they were punched in the face. They shut down. They can't talk to anyone. They feel that sting of rejection in their chest and are constantly reliving the painful experience in their mind. They are emotionally drained after one tiny tap to their ego.

It takes energy to constantly manage the image you present to the world. By trying to protect yourself in this way it often just makes you weaker and more prone to rejection.

By integrating the rejected parts of yourself you can improve your emotional health and feel more energetic because you won't be wasting energy on trying to influence what people think about you. You will just present yourself to the world and not be bothered by people who aren't interested in who you really are.

The inability to accept yourself is what causes the fear of rejection and leads you to worry about wearing cool clothes, saying the right thing and presenting yourself in a way that people will accept. Self-acceptance clearly helps you develop a more mature authentic self.

Chapter 5: How to Develop Self-acceptance

"Because one believes in oneself, one doesn't try to convince others. Because one is content with oneself, one doesn't need others' approval. Because one accepts oneself, the whole world accepts him or her."
— **Lao Tzu**

Neutrality allows you to keep an open mind. It prevents you from being judgmental and overreacting to the thoughts you need to confront.

When you begin you should start with a calm mind. This is why it can be helpful to deal with these issues when you are in a good mood. It would feel even worse to deal with them when you are in a downward spiral of negativity and you could encounter more resistance within yourself.

Neutrality opens you up to compassion for yourself. You don't need to hate the darker parts of your personality as social pressure might lead you to believe. When you are overly critical of yourself it only increases shame and other neurotic tendencies.

The parts of yourself you are ashamed of need as much acceptance as the positive parts that receive social approval. Acceptance of anger doesn't mean you need to become a violent person. Acceptance of intelligence doesn't mean you need to become an arrogant know it all. Acceptance of your sexuality doesn't mean you'll become a slut. Acceptance only means you give permission to these parts of yourself to exist. You no longer need to waste energy running away from yourself. With acceptance comes the process of balancing opposing desires.

Have compassion for yourself. Realize that you are only critical of some aspects of your personality because social pressure has brainwashed you to be ashamed of them.

Recognize that social pressure isn't some evil force designed to keep you in a nightmarish hell of pain and limiting beliefs.

In reality it is an integral part of the human experience and pushes both you and society in the right direction as we all collectively attempt to balance selfish desires with compassion for each other. It's vital to be aware of this often chaotic process.

Develop Self-Awareness

Without self-awareness you won't realize what bad habits are sabotaging your progress towards confidence and other life goals. As mentioned previously, reflecting on your experiences is essential to changing destructive behaviors.

A common suggestion for the development of self-awareness is to practice mindfulness meditation. Mindfulness means you pay attention to how your body feels, the thoughts you are thinking, and other elements within your immediate environment. This is a practice in staying aware of the present moment.

Developing self-awareness helps you observe and evaluate your emotional reactions and experiences without value judgments such as "good" or "bad."

Maintaining awareness of your emotional state helps prevent anger and frustrations from impeding your progress. You are able to deal with these reactions more maturely.

Self-awareness helps you understand your strengths and weaknesses so you know what you need to work on and make progress towards your goals.

Be Honest

Being honest with yourself should go without saying.

This means confronting some very undesirable traits and experiences. It won't be easy or comfortable.

People invest a huge amount of energy to prevent others from seeing this hidden side of themselves. This effort can be so convincing that people often fool themselves and don't realize how much denial they are actually in.

It takes courage to admit to negative thoughts, bad habits, and destructive desires. The results are worth enduring the discomfort as you reexamine lost parts of yourself.

You must also take responsibility for acknowledging every part of yourself you may have suppressed. There are too many possibilities to list them all here. It will take real self-honesty and willingness to recognize many of these.

Record Your Insights

Writing about your insights helps you develop self-awareness. You can review your discoveries at a later date and continue where you left off.

You don't need to write down every detail. However, whenever you have a breakthrough or realize there is something you should resolve it can be helpful to take a note of it.

It's usually more helpful to write by hand in a notebook you have dedicated to your own self-improvement. Of course if you insist you can also record your insights on your phone or computer.

After a few months of this practice you can review these insights and realize the progress you have actually made. Taking a few minutes a day a few times a week will be worth it.

Observe your emotional reactions

The disowned self is ashamed to exist.

You subconsciously hide it to keep it out of view. The more you pay attention to your behaviors and emotional reactions the more you will observe these disowned aspects compensating for the lack of approval.

Pay especially close attention to when other people disappoint, annoy and anger you. These reactions are often projections of parts of yourself you want to run away from.

When negative emotional reactions occur it rarely seems appropriate to analyze these feelings. You get lost in the emotion and it can consume your thoughts for as long as you let it. It can however be more productive to ask yourself, "Why do I feel this way?" and analyze the thoughts that emerge.

Some say whatever irritates you in other people is something you've disowned in yourself. There is a way to find out. When someone does something that irritates you, honestly assess if part of you would enjoy doing the same thing.

Maybe you see someone yelling angrily or showing off for attention, ask yourself if you are ever guilty of wanting to do the same thing. Accept that part of yourself and try to understand it.

Next time you encounter it in someone else you likely will react with more compassion and less agitation.

Ask yourself these questions:

What causes emotional reactions in you?

What makes you angry?

What makes you sad?

What disappoints you?

What hurts you?

When do you feel disrespected?

Honestly answering these questions will help you realize parts of yourself you may be denying.

Identify Imbalances in Your Personality

Social pressure compels us to be "good" people in order to survive. The definition of "good" becomes whatever is acceptable within society.

"Good" is a relative term for whatever is acceptable at a given time and place. Absolute good and bad is a philosophical question that is very challenging to answer.

Write down a list of your most positive traits. Then next to these traits write down the opposite and try to identify it within yourself. Take a moment to contemplate each trait. In what ways might you be suppressing that negative trait? When might you have projected it onto others?

If you identify as a very considerate person you could be repressing selfish desires. If you identify as very serious you could be repressing the part of you that wants to relax and express a sense of humor.

To compensate for an area we lack we might lean too far in the opposite direction. If your parents always responded to your humor with negativity you may have hidden that part of yourself to gain their approval. To ensure your survival you became as serious as possible. You began to hate humor, dirty jokes and became overly sensitive to everything you consider inappropriate.

The disowned parts of your subconscious are triggered whenever you engage in or see inconsiderate or humorous behavior. Whenever you feel like acting selfishly or telling a dirty joke you feel guilty for even considering it. Recognize your own examples and accept them.

You know which parts of yourself you have hidden or pretend don't even exist. Acknowledge them without criticism.

Aim for Balance

The goal of self-acceptance is to balance opposing qualities. This helps you react appropriately in social situations, reconnect with your innate happiness, and to express yourself more confidently.

Balance means you can benefit from both sides of a spectrum. For example, if you are an extreme follower you will be afraid to make decisions when it matters to you.

If you are a tyrannical leader you might refuse to listen to great advice from someone on your team.

If you are a follower and are intimidated by confident leaders it may be time to embrace that side of yourself.

If you are an arrogant and bossy person it might be time to develop some listening skills and show actual curiosity in other people. By recognizing the side you've rejected in yourself you move closer to it and will be less threatened by it.

In the previous exercise you examined some opposing qualities based on positive traits you are proud of. This gives you a taste of what areas you need to work on balancing.

Let's look at more traits that might need similar attention within yourself. These are based on emotions, behaviors, habits, and social conditioning.

Obviously with most of these you will lean a little left or right. Take note any qualities that really irritate you when you see it in others. It is likely a sign you've disowned that quality in yourself and it deserves recognition and acceptance to achieve balance.

Victor ←→ Victim

When you play games do you always feel the need to win?

Are you obsessed with succeeding at everything you do? Or do you secretly enjoy failure because it means you can gain some pity and attention?

Are you ambitious or lazy?

We have already discussed how to overcome the victim mentality. These self-described victims have rejected the winner within themselves.

Balanced, the victor is willing to graciously accept defeat and the victim recognizes his own potential for success.

Controlling Tyrant ←→ **Carefree/careless**

Do you try to take control of all situations?

Do you always have to be the leader and dominate decisions within your teams? Or are you afraid of making decisions for fear they will be judged? Or do you just not care enough?

When these two are balanced you are capable of making decisions you care about and don't freak out when you don't get your way.

Liar ←→ **Innocent Child**

Do you ever manipulate others to get your way? Do you exaggerate or alter the truth to win people over to your side? Do you lie to impress people or manage what they think of you? Such as your age, occupation, etc. Or are you an innocent child obsessed with always doing the right thing? Are you excessively direct and honest?

When balanced the impulse to manipulate will be drastically reduced and honest statements can be delivered more tactfully.

Selfish ←→ Selfless

Balancing these two is an essential part of developing into a mature adult. As we've discussed already, leaning too far in either of these directions can have life threatening consequences.

What triggers you to be the most selfish? How do you justify your selfishness?

What triggers your selfless and considerate side? Sometimes you need to be a little selfish. Sometimes you need to offer compassion to your fellow human being.

Individual ←→ Conformist

Are you creative and fashionable? Or do you wear the same clothes everyone else is wearing? Are you brave enough to express ideas that don't conform to the mainstream narrative? Or do you believe whatever those around you believe without questioning it? The extreme individual may be an outcast. It is however possible he is admired for his eccentric style as he conforms to enough rules to maintain acceptance. The extreme conformist doesn't have a single original idea in his mind. He has rejected every attempt his individuality has made to emerge.

It is up to you to decide how much individuality you want to develop versus how many social norms you want to abide by. It's ok to question some of the rules society has thrust upon you. It's equally ok to withhold your personal style at appropriate times. It's more likely an imbalance here causes conformist tendencies. So figure out how much of your personality you have been suppressing.

Independent ←→ Codependent

Do you do whatever you want? Or do you need the support of others to take action? People in codependent relationships may feel they can't accept themselves so need approval of others.

Codependents have difficulty respecting each other's individuality and are afraid of separation. They can't tolerate disagreement and have difficulty taking responsibility for their own actions.

When balanced you can achieve interdependency. This means you maintain healthy relationships in which all people involved respect each other's individuality and freedom.

It's easier to be upfront and honest in these relationships as your sense of self-worth isn't dependent on the relationship but rather adds value to it.

Quiet ←→ Talkative

If you are reading a book on confidence chances are you might be suppressing the side of you that wants to be more expressive. It's also possible very chatty people have been encouraged to contribute more to conversations and consequently have a fear of awkward silences. When balanced you can appreciate both conversation and silence.

Patient pushover ←→ impatient dominator

If someone yelled at you, would you patiently wait for them to go away or would you yell back even louder? Do you allow people to take advantage of you or do you swiftly take revenge for your hurt feelings? When balanced you can wait patiently when necessary and you won't be as sensitive to minor inconveniences. You will also be able to stand up for yourself when you need to.

Humility ←→ Arrogance

Does praise bother you or does it feed your ego? Being too humble prevents others from appreciating what's great about you because they never hear about it. It also makes you more likely to be a follower rather than a leader. Too much arrogance betrays underlying insecurity.

Arrogance and pride are a weak form of confidence. This poor man's courage makes you more sensitive to insult. It's as if you climbed to the top of the ladder and you are shouting about how awesome you are. Then someone criticizes your accomplishment and you jump down from the ladder into anger and beat them up or go home and cry. A confident person wouldn't feel the need to react at all. They know if they've actually accomplished something great or not and they don't require recognition to feel validation. They are internally validated.

If you have too much humility you may have a fear of being seen as arrogant. When balanced you can appreciate your accomplishments without bragging.

Perfectionist ←→ Lazy slob

Do you always stick to a strict schedule or do you procrastinate more than you should? The overly perfectionist refuses to indulge in pleasures or waste time. They can in fact accomplish a lot, however they feel guilty about the slightest lapse in their willpower. The lazy slob doesn't care about schedules and often procrastinates. The extreme lazy slob may be irritated at uptight perfectionists. When balanced self-discipline can be maintained but still afford occasional indulgences.

Optimist ←→ Pessimist

Do smiley happy people piss you off? Why are they so happy? Do negative people kill your vibe? Optimism feels great, but sometimes it isn't always realistic. Pessimists and optimists have a lot they can teach each other. When balanced you can see the world more clearly and react more appropriately.

Rude ←→ Too polite

Do have zero concern for how your words and actions affect others? Or are you so worried about hurting people's feelings that you abstain from expressing the truth?

Do rude people make you hurt and angry? You may be suppressing your rude/direct side.

Do polite people seem fake to you? You may be hiding the side of you that wants to show concern for others. When balanced you can express yourself directly without being rude.

Promiscuous ←→ Chaste / Loyal

Are you afraid of being seen as a slut but secretly have many sexual desires? This is very common in religious communities. In fact statistics show that porn consumption is the highest in countries and communities that are the most sexually repressed. The more you hide a desire the more it will influence your thoughts and behavior.

Conversely if you are extremely promiscuous you may be using sex to fill emotional holes and are afraid of commitment and losing the various benefits of sexual attention. When balanced you can have guilt free sexual relationships but also be willing to commit to a monogamous relationship.

How to Balance Imbalances

If you only lean a little left or right on the above spectrums you shouldn't need to worry about finding balance. The more you lean one direction in a spectrum the more its opposite will annoy or frighten you. It's time for you to examine why that is.

The following steps will help you face and integrate these opposing parts of your identity you may have been too frightened of to admit even exist.

Step 1:

Choose the area in which you may be overcompensating for disowned traits. Such as if you are a very quiet person maybe overly talkative people make you uncomfortable. This suggests you've rejected the talkative/expressive part of yourself.

Choose a person or situation that irritates or upsets you in relation to this trait. Perhaps a relative or coworker is too chatty or has some other behavior that triggers a strong emotional reaction within you.

Step 2:

Visualize this person and pinpoint the details that upset you the most. Write down your emotions or at least discuss them with yourself

Step 3:

Change the memory.

Talk to the person whose actions upset you as if they were actually present.

Tell them exactly what you want to say.

Ask them questions such as these:

- Why are you doing that?
- What do you want?
- Why do you behave differently than I would in the same situation?
- What can I learn from this?

Allow your imagination to provide answers to your questions. It will be even more effective if you record this conversation in writing.

Step 4:

Trade places. This is the most uncomfortable part. It is also the most essential. Pretend you've traded places with this person and you see things from their perspective. If you are a quiet non-confrontational person maybe you step into the shoes of an angry and loud person who doesn't mind causing a scene.

See the situation as they see it. Ask yourself questions to figure out the motivations of this perspective.

Why do you shout angrily?

Why don't you care what people think of you? Answers will emerge from your imagination.

Describe yourself in this new perspective:

- I am loud
- I am angry.
- I am rude
- I am ambitious
- I am humble

The more uncomfortable this is the more you have likely disowned these traits.

Step 5:

Acknowledge these disowned traits in yourself. Remember specific experiences in which you have felt and behaved in the same ways as the people who upset you. Accept that this same trait does actually exist within you too. Don't be ashamed of it. Accept it and even find something pleasurable in exploring this side of yourself. This will allow you to re-own it. Take as long as needed to go through each of your unbalanced traits several times with this exercise.

Connect with your Authenticity

In the previous exercises you have been asked to confront a part of yourself you may have forgotten even existed. You may hide negative emotions like sadness, fear, and embarrassment because you worry people will reject you if you express these honestly. The truth however is that people crave authenticity and are disgusted by inauthenticity. When you can express yourself honestly people recognize their own humanity within you. But when you try to impress others, or pretend something isn't bothering you it only prevents them from trusting you.

When some people feel like pretending they don't care about an incident that makes them feel terrible they might laugh or retort with a silly comeback. However this reaction is only serves to hide what is really going on inside. Maybe he finally he his hero. A man he looks up to. But the hero is very rude. He will respond politely, or laugh because he respects this hero but he is only hiding how he really feels.

Through social conditioning we develop an inauthentic façade we present to the world in order to survive. As mentioned, this starts in childhood when we are criticized for crying in public, anger, are interested in things we enjoy but others disapprove of, or any emotion or behavior that doesn't meet the standards of others.

We quickly learn what behaviors, beliefs and attitudes are acceptable. You then filter all your behaviors and statements to make sure you never say or do anything that isn't on the approved list of acceptability.

This is awesome for society. People are more likely to follow rules and acceptable norms of behavior that keep communities running smoothly. Even though you might like to run into a candy store and eat your fill without paying that impulse will be accompanied by a stronger compulsion shouting, "No you can't do that! You'd be punished, and hated by other people!"

That is the very beginning of morality. People don't automatically do the right thing because it's the right thing. They need to be pushed into that direction by threats of rejection or pain. This has a lot of potential to keep society alive and thriving. However, it equally has the potential to cause people to do incredibly evil acts when they are just following orders.

So being social animals the weight of social pressure inclines us to do whatever is popular among our peers. We worry about losing their approval and in general do whatever is required to maintain that approval. This makes connection with your authentic self challenging.

Authenticity is what you are. It's not something you need to pursue. You already have it. To reconnect with it you need to turn off the filter which constantly makes you ask yourself, *"Is this socially acceptable?"*

You might want to go talk to a cute girl and think, *"Is it ok if I say hi?"*

You might want to wear a colorful shirt you love but think, *"Would this shirt make me look weird?"*

You may be having a very nice day. You are walking down the street and an inconsiderate jerk walking the opposite directing pushes into you almost knocking you over. You are pissed off inside. You might want to shout at him to watch where he's going but then your imagination will be filled with the scene of people nearby getting bothered by your loud voice and staring at you and you'll think, *"Oh shit! I can't do that!"*

That nagging voice is there to ensure the survival of the human race. It doesn't want you to succeed. It doesn't want you to become the most amazing version of yourself possible. That would be too risky. If it can prevent you from engaging in enough dangerous situations maybe you will survive long enough to pass on your genes.

Everybody has this filter. The problem is the socially anxious have turned this feature on super high because approval has become top priority. They hold onto this filter strongly because they worry letting go of it would be suicide. The more you allow this filter to control your behavior the worse you will feel.

It might be confusing when you want to turn off the filter. Many people, companies, brands, and even friends try to keep up a polite front to make you happy. People will constantly wear a fake smile and tell you what you want to hear.

Does it feel good to live in a thick layer of bullshit? Obviously there are times when tact and proper etiquette are necessary. But if you really think about it the most meaningful moments of your life are those where you felt true authenticity. Getting to know a new person without trying to impress them, a thoughtful compliment, sharing embarrassing stories, all require realness and disengaging the bullshit filter.

The more authenticity in your life the easier it will be to turn off this filter. If you are surrounded by authentic people will feel the pressure to be real with them if you want to gain their acceptance.

It feels good to encounter authentic people. It's easier to trust them. It feels safe to say anything you want. We naturally respond to it positively. When we encounter inauthentic people in can leave a dirty taste in your soul.

Enduring inauthenticity is a result of forgetting how to be yourself. If you aren't comfortable being yourself, you will allow social pressure to mold you into a typical worker bee with hardly a trace of original personality left. Your authentic self will remain dormant until you acknowledge and let it break free of the chains of the bullshit filter.

Authentic people are attractive. They don't worry about what other people think of them because they are internally validated. They get their emotions from within, not from praise and approval of others. This confidence draws people to them. If they are free of worries it must be a sign their life is great. On the other hand, when you feel like you aren't good enough it can cause you to engage your bullshit filter.

This obviously makes you very inauthentic as you desperately need approval to feel worthy of other people.

This pushes people away. The more socially intelligent a person is the more disgusted they will be by inauthenticity.

When a date, party, or any social interaction goes well it's usually because we allowed our authenticity to flow. When you prefer inauthenticity it's because you are not yet comfortable being yourself.

Inauthenticity can be mimicking the words and actions of the people around you. It can also be a deep feeling of inadequacy that prevents you from expressing your real thoughts and emotions.

Many people need to maintain a polite though deceptive front for work. This work persona may be terrified about revealing any detail about your real identity. You present an acceptable vanilla shell to coworkers and customers because you feel your survival depends on keeping this job. If however you were living in abundance and felt there were plenty of opportunities if you lost your job it might actually help you relax and not worry as much. People also use the same strategies in relationships. They even lie to friends.

When you are accustomed to this being authentic seems increasingly scary. The more you hide the more you will sabotage yourself. For example, guys feeling extremely nervous may pretend they are legends. They wake up in the morning and repeat to themselves, "I'm a confident badass!" They start conversations by mimicking the words and actions of a badass. But if they don't have sufficient self-belief they only come across as insecure. Compare this to a shy guy who starts conversations by admitting he is nervous. This often results in great reactions because socially intelligent people, especially women, are experts at detecting authenticity. The low self-esteem self-described badass quickly dismisses this approach. He assumes he always needs to project confidence, fearlessness and perfection. He can't admit he's nervous because he's afraid people will think it's weak and reject him. The best approach is always honesty.

It's time to turn off that bullshit filter. Pay attention to when that filter discourages you from taking an action you know deep down you want to try. Your instinct to give in to the filter will be strong. It might cause you to choke up and not be able to speak or move. Accept the fear and do it anyway.

When you feel tempted to pretend you like something you actually hate, tolerate rude behavior, or agree to an obligation you don't actually care about take pleasure in this realization. It's an opportunity to reconnect with your authenticity.

You become authentic again by removing all the bullshit from how you communicate and present yourself to the world. Throw out the approval seeking compliments, illogical ideas you only pretended to believe in, pretending you care, pretending you don't care, and everything else that gets in the way. If you have humorous phrases you constantly repeat because you know they always get positive reactions it's time to forget about them for a while. You don't need them to be authentic and experience a real human connection. Don't worry. When you are willing to be authentic and live in the moment your creativity will flow and you should know what to say anyway. When you subtract these things you will be left with authenticity.

What happens if people see you sad? You might think people think you aren't good enough and they'll reject you. You think it's unacceptable to show your real thoughts and emotions but people actually crave that authenticity. When you let go of resistance you'll finally be comfortable being you.

You are scared of saying the wrong thing. But as soon as you say what you really want that fear disappears. Show your weakness, frustration, and sadness. You'll realize nothing bad happens and people can appreciate it.

Chapter 6: Accepting Anxious Feelings

"To venture causes anxiety, but not to venture is to lose one's self... And to venture in the highest is to be conscious of one's self."
— **Soren Kierkegaard**

You may realize anxious feelings are illogical but these negative emotions still inhibit your behavior. You might want to start a conversation with a cute new coworker but you might feel a pain in your chest, you might blush, feel a general sense of dread as you seriously consider starting a conversation. To avoid this uncomfortable feeling you completely forget about getting to know your coworker and a few weeks later find out some other loser you work with is dating her.

Take a moment to think about your own experience of wanting to interact with another person but then deciding not to because the pain of anxiety was too strong. Does this really make sense? It's a little funny if you think about it. You know the words you wanted to say but they just wouldn't come out. You had the capacity to socialize but some negative feeling made you scared of something that came with zero risk at all.

In his book The Flinch, Julien Smith uses this common fear response as a metaphor for all anxieties. He writes, "Behind every act you're unable to do, fear of the flinch is there, like a puppet master, steering you off course. Facing the flinch is hard. It means seeing the lies you tell yourself, facing the fear behind them, and handling the pain that your journey demands—all without hesitation. The flinch is the moment every doubt you've ever had comes back and hits you, hard. It's when your body feels tense. It's an instinct that tells you to run. It's a moment of tension that happens in the body and the brain, and it stops everything cold."

Smith rightly explains that even though "the flinch" exists to protect you, it's necessary to handle this emotional response or you could fall prey to outside forces. The flinch is the anticipation of pain that might not even exist. It's the uncomfortable anticipation you might feel before entering cold water. Before you are about to step in you will feel the resistance. Assuming you aren't already used to cold showers of course. But if you step into the water, after a few moments you can get used to it.

Cold showers actually have a lot of health benefits, and increase awareness. Even though you anticipated discomfort, it would likely feel good afterwards. The only reason you dreaded going into the cold water was because you weren't used to it. There weren't even any negative consequences.

It will be the same with most social interactions that cause you anxiety. When you accept your emotional reactions you can train yourself to react with more congruence to what is important to you.

We have been discussing acceptance and by now you see the value of accepting parts of your identity you have suppressed.

Working on this has helped many people relieve intense anxieties. But anxious feelings will still prevent you from exiting your comfort zone.

To combat this I've included some exercises in this section that build awareness and acceptance of these feelings.

Part 1: Body Mindfulness meditation

Daily meditation for at least 10 minutes a day can change your life. We've already discussed how meditation can help you disconnect from the distractions and addictions of everyday life to help you rediscover internal validation.

This activity will be a little different. It involves bringing attention to the various parts of the body. The goal of this practice is to increase awareness of the sensations in the body. Many people are unconscious of these sensations. They are happening all the time. Some may be obvious. Such as the heavy feeling in your head and eyes when you are exhausted and the body needs sleep. Ignore this signal and you will either be tired and unable to concentrate or eventually start seeing hallucinations. There are always consequences to ignoring these signals. Unfortunately some of these signals may be very subtle and difficult to recognize if they have been chronic so long you assume it is just your usual state.

Many people who are tired all the time assume it's just the way they are instead of examining their sleeping and other lifestyle habits. People suffering from social anxiety often don't realize the low hum of fear that is constantly sending signals to the brain to release low levels of cortisol and other stress hormones.

This exercise isn't to control these emotional signals. It's only to help you recognize them.

Sit in a comfortable position with your back straight. Take 10 deep breaths one after the other. Inhale quickly. Exhale normally. If you must you can lay down at this point. Avoid moving as much as possible.

With your eyes closed start paying attention to your breathing. Breathe normally.

Don't control it.

Just experience it.

Notice how your body expands on the inhale and contracts on the exhale.

Next move your awareness to your toes. Spend a moment on that spot before concentrating on the entire foot. Slowly move awareness up the body as you go. How does that part of the body feel? Warm, cool, sore, stiff, itchy, etc.

Spend a few breaths on each part of your body before shifting awareness. If you have recently been feeling social anxiety try to find where that emotion is located in your body. If it is uncomfortable to accept these negative feelings it will require practice.

Part 2: Accepting Anxious Feelings

I. What sensations do you feel when you encounter social situations you are afraid of? Examples may be dry mouth, sweating, racing heart rate, shaking, blushing, chest discomfort, a choking sensation in the throat preventing you from speaking etc.

II. Accept these sensations. With your eyes closed, imagine an anxiety inducing situation. It could be a memory or a usual social situation that you would like to feel more confident in. Imagine the situation is even scarier than usual. What sensations do you feel and where? Make a decision to accept these sensations. If this becomes too intense you can take a break and continue the next day. Let go of urges to ignore or change these uncomfortable feelings.

III. Record your experiences. When you encounter social anxiety what do you feel and where? How is your progress to accepting these sensations instead of resisting them?

These sensations are the body's way of encouraging you to avoid risk. Risk is determined by your own imagination combined with the habits of your previous experience.

If you've always assumed meeting new people contains a risk of rejection that baseless assumption will trigger these sensations that encourage you to protect yourself from all the horrific dangers of saying, "Hi!" to a new person.

By accepting these sensations in social situations it eventually helps you to stop unnecessarily labeling interactions as risky.

Now that you know how to develop awareness of your anxious feelings it's time to start practicing regularly if you actually want results.

For at least 10 consecutive days practice this mindfulness exercise. If you work on strengthening your acceptance you will likely feel more energetic and positive in social situations.

You can practice this any time of the day. It might be helpful to do them at a regular time.

What's better for you morning or night? You could go to bed about 15 minutes earlier than usual and practice this exercise.

You can then think about the anxiety inducing experiences of the day. Where and what did you feel?

You'll need to make a choice to invest in yourself. Experiment with this exercise for a couple weeks and pay attention to the difference it makes in your life in combination with the other suggestions throughout this book.

Chapter 7: How to Overcome Social Anxiety

"Man is not worried by real problems so much as by his imagined anxieties about real problems."

— **Epictetus**

When we examine our disowned traits we look deep inside ourselves to see the roots of our fearful behavior and attempt to balance incongruities. Now we look at the external behaviors our fear of social situations manifest.

The spectrum of social anxiety can begin at mild shyness and go all the way to severe Avoidant Personality Disorder. No matter how extreme, social anxiety connects to fears of being observed, judged, embarrassed, or rejected.

How to love all social interactions

Talking with people is inevitable. People will randomly say annoying things to you. People will suddenly ask personal questions you don't want to answer. You'll need to attend social events. People will intimidate you. And obviously there are many interactions required in our daily lives to ensure everyone's survival. If you have to do it, you might as well find a way to enjoy it. At the very least you can accept these inevitabilities. The more you resist them the more you will avoid situations required to develop maturity and confidence.

Shyness often depends on who you are talking to, your role, the ages of people involved and other factors you might not even be consciously aware of. To help you overcome the specific fears that trigger your own social anxiety, take a moment to answer the following questions:

1. Who triggers your social anxiety?
   - Coworkers
   - Your boss / manager
   - Acquaintances
   - Strangers
   - Friends
   - Authority figures such as police, doctor, employer etc.
   - Family members
   - People you would like to date
   - People who intimidate you
   - People physically larger than you
   - People who never smile
   - People who dress differently than you (more professional/ more fashionable etc.)
   - People who seem more successful than you
   - People you want to impress
   - One person
   - A group of people
   - Neighbors
   - Salespeople
   - Other:_____

2. When talking to people, what triggers anxiety for you?

- Starting a conversation
- Ending a conversation
- Sharing personal information
- Superficial small talk (weather, news, etc.)
- Not knowing what to say
- Expressing your honest opinion, especially when it conflicts with what the other person said.
- Inviting someone to a date
- Speaking on the phone
- Asking for help
- Trying to impress others
- Making a suggestion (Where to eat, what to do etc.)
- Waiting for a positive reaction (smile, asking follow up question etc.)
- Asking boring questions you don't even really want to ask to keep the conversation going
- Making a request
- Disagreeing
- Expressing anger or dissatisfaction
- Other:_____

Looking at your answers to these two questions you can have a clear image of what specific people and actions trigger your social anxiety. Write these down so you can develop awareness of the situations you should work on. The situations and individuals to trigger your fear response will be unique to your own life experience. Some people may dread boring small talk with coworkers but have zero fear of starting conversations with beautiful strangers. Others might be socially fearless with coworkers and most people but stutter and shake nervously when they try to talk to someone they are romantically interested in.

Judgement Fear

If starting conversations still seems terrifying, there may be less obvious fears you should first address. Such as the fear of being observed and judged by others. If you are afraid of any of the following then make a note of it in your progress journal:

- Waiting in line
- Making eye contact with strangers
- Public transportation
- Eating in front of others
- Drinking in front of others
- Reading in front of others

- Writing in front of others
- Talking on the phone in public
- Using a crowded elevator
- Exercising in front of others
- Doing work that involves being observed by others

Performance anxiety

The fear of being judged can apply to any situation. Performance anxiety is a bit higher pressure as it can involve the risk of messing up. Everyone is paying attention to you and it's your turn to deliver what they expect. It's common to feel judged in these situations if you haven't practiced them.

What performance situations trigger your anxiety?

- Public speaking
- Giving a Presentation, speech, demonstration etc.
- Dancing in public
- Performing a skill you can do well if practiced alone but often fail at in public because of anxiety
- Taking a test
- Introducing yourself to a group of people
- Asking a question at a meeting
- Singing in front of others

- Being interviewed
- Asking questions / speaking when other people will overhear what you say
- Acting
- Sports competition
- Playing a game
- Playing a musical instrument
- Recording a video of yourself
- Counting money/change
- Making a complaint
- Artistic performance in public
- Talking to customers
- Cooperating on a group project
- Other _____

As you can see there are 3 distinct types of situations that can trigger social anxiety. Examine how conversation anxiety, general fear of being judged, and performance anxiety are problematic in your life.

Choose the 5 most anxiety inducing social situations.

Example:

1. Starting conversations with strangers
2. Sharing personal information
3. First dates
4. Public speaking

5. Not knowing what to say

The following questions and exercises will help you examine why these situations cause you so much unnecessary anxiety and help you think of ways to overcome them.

Let's now look at several key factors involved in causing problems in these areas.

The Comfort Zone

To survive we obviously need safety. Psychologists agree that social anxiety likely has its utility in helping people survive. After all, if everyone was super confident they'd all take dangerous risks until our species was extinct. Fear and avoidance of danger is therefore completely natural. We instinctually find a comfort zone and protect it like an eagle protecting her nest. The size of the comfort zone of course depends on the person. Just because yours may be very small now doesn't mean it always needs to be.

When you establish your comfort zone anytime you reach its edge anxiety causes you to resist and pull away.

You will naturally develop habits that keep you feeling safe. Examples of these comfort zone habits are always letting friends order for you when you go to restaurants because you are afraid to speak to the waitress, or always staying with your friend when you go to a party because you are afraid to be alone.

Many people strictly avoid any social situation that could cause even the hint of anxiety. It may seem like a genius plan to avoid talking to cute strangers in order to avoid rejection but you would only be missing out on opportunities to develop social skills and reestablish the limits of your comfort zone. Living like this is not living at all.

Every opportunity you avoid, invitation you turn down shrinks the edge of the comfort zone. Insist on this type of behavior and you risk developing avoidant personality disorder and being terrified of even leaving your home.

Think of social situations you have avoided. What was the negative impact of this avoidance?

For example, you might want to go to some parties to make new friends, but you constantly cancel your plans to do this. The negative impact could be you continue to feel lonely, bored, and depressed.

Maybe you were tasked with giving a speech at work. You practiced, but still felt too scared to perform. You pretend you are sick and cancel it. You missed an opportunity to develop your public speaking skills, confidence, and to convince your boss you are responsible and worthy of a promotion. Try to use the 5 situations you have already written down if you can.

Socially anxious people are often ashamed of themselves. This inadequacy comes out in shy, self-conscious behavior. Such as avoiding eye contact, stuttering, speaking too quietly, etc. To hide both this shame and its symptoms they will adopt sneaky behaviors.

Be honest with yourself and you might realize you are guilty of some of these yourself. Here are some of the typical behaviors:

- *In conversation:* Asking lots of questions to avoid talking about yourself. Speaking quickly to say as much as possible without being interrupted. Fear of silence. Pauses in conversation make them feel anxious and they rush to fill it with something. Preparing topics instead of spontaneous conversation.

- *To hide anxiety:* wearing makeup, especially too much is often a sign someone isn't confident in their appearance. Holding a glass in front of the chest. Wearing an extra layer of clothes to hide nervous sweating.

- *In Social events:* Never leaving your friend's side. Staring at your phone pretending you have something important to do.

- *In Public:* Staring at your phone, avoiding eye contact, keeping distance between yourself and others, always getting out of everyone's way.

- *Disagreement avoidance:* Always agreeing, smiling, never complaining, and never revealing a conflicting opinion.

- *Attention avoidance:* Sitting in the back of a room, remaining as quiet as possible, begrudgingly doing whatever task you have been assigned without complaint.

- *Dating:* Always agreeing with everything your date says. Pretending to be impressed with things that might not even deserve it. Excessive complimenting instead of playful teasing.

If you are guilty of some of these don't worry. If you look for them you will see this type of anxiety avoidance is very common. And at least people engaging in these behaviors are trying to socialize even if they do so with this fear induced crutch.

However these behaviors still limit your ability to build real social connections and enjoy life. It's like you are a bird and you've been pushed out of the nest by big momma eagle. Instead of soaring away into the stratosphere you are clinging to the branch of these anxiety avoidance behaviors. If you only let go you could realize you actually have a pair of wings and already know how to fly instinctually. It's only the fear of flying that prevents you from actually doing it.

Take a moment to recognize your own anxiety avoidance behaviors. Be honest with yourself about why you do these things.

You might feel relief when you successfully avoid what you perceive to be a potentially anxiety inducing situation. But seriously ask yourself:

What are you giving up for that relief?

Write down at least one of these behaviors for each of your 5 most anxiety inducing situations.

Example:

Anxiety trigger: First dates

Anxiety avoidance behavior in this situation: Planning a list of questions before the date to avoid awkward silence triggering anxiety.

Negative impact of this behavior: Remaining fearful of spontaneous conversation and silent tension. Reinforces lack of confidence in your social skills.

List as many of these avoidance behaviors for each of your feared situations as possible. Follow this by contemplating and writing down the negative impact these behaviors have on your life. This will help you understand the real cost of avoidance.

Observe your Anxiety

Notice which situations make you worry about embarrassing yourself.

Focusing on the risk of encountering anxiety inducing situations will only intensify your negative feelings and the impulse to engage in avoidant behaviors will increase.

Logically you may realize the person looking at you is not likely to approach or speak to you. However you still feel an urge to avoid eye contact and run away.

Now that you are aware of which fears and behaviors are feeding your lack of social success you can devise a plan to transform these fears and expand your comfort zone. These behaviors hurt you much more than they help you. It's important to see that. If you focus on the benefits of changing these avoidant behaviors you will be much more likely to develop more beneficial habits.

How to change these bad habits

Every time you tighten your grip on the branch of avoidant behavior you reinforce negative thoughts of inadequacy, and lose opportunities to develop confidence. These processes usually occur subconsciously. But now that you are aware of them you can either take responsibility for your actions or feel even more like a loser because you know it's possible to change if you tried.

Giving up now would be like Neo choosing the red pill in the Matrix, realizing the truth of reality, getting scared and then pretending to go back to his blue pill existence in the make believe computer simulation. He might be able to lie to himself that it's more comfortable this way, but he is only hiding from reality and denying the truth.

Replacing avoidant behaviors with more confident ones isn't as easy as taking a magic pill that opens your eyes to reality. But it can similarly lead you to liberating realizations.

Let's examine how habits are formed and take advantage of this process to build more confident habits. Habits are basically formed in 3 steps:

1. **Trigger**: Outside event triggers social anxiety. Such as starting a conversation, someone suddenly asking you a question, or making a phone call

2. **Reaction:** The avoidant behavior that comes with the anxious response. Such as cancelling invitations, speaking too quietly, and running away from social situations.

3. **Reward:** The feeling of relief you get from the avoidant behavior.

You should already realize by now that the "reward" of relief you get from avoidant behavior should be viewed as negative and detrimental to your confidence. Now that you are aware of you can take responsibility for your reactions to them. You will feel the urge to do your usual avoidance behavior but that is exactly when you should adopt a new more positive reaction.

For example, if every time coworkers ask you questions you feel anxious and react by avoiding eye contact, speaking very little and then exiting the conversation as quickly as possible you can make a conscious effort to change this reaction to more eye contact, asking questions back to your coworkers, and staying in the conversation as long as possible. At first this may feel awkward because you aren't chasing the reward of relief in your usual avoidant way. However you can still convince yourself that these new behaviors are even more rewarding.

To make this even more effective you can use consistent rewarding behavior every time you react more confidently than usual. Such as eating a piece of chocolate or something similar.

Eventually you will form new habits that looks closer to this:

1. **Trigger:** Starting conversations with new people.

2. **Reaction:** The avoidant reaction might be to think of excuses to avoid speaking to someone. "They look busy." "I don't look cool enough today" etc. And then give up on socializing. Replace this reaction with always saying

something to new people. At least "Hi" and a follow up statement or question is enough. You don't need people to give you an amazing reaction.

3. **Reward:** relief from realization it's acceptable and even enjoyable to start conversations with new people, eating a piece of chocolate, or something else you enjoy.

The new reactions will eventually become your usual response to these triggers. Every time you react appropriately you reinforce positive habits that help you develop both inner and outer confidence. You will be more comfortable in these social situations and more capable of interacting with others.

Chapter 8: Limiting Beliefs

"Never surrender your hopes and dreams to the fateful limitations others have placed on their own lives. The vision of your true destiny does not reside within the blinkered outlook of the naysayers and the doom prophets. Judge not by their words, but accept advice based on the evidence of actual results. Do not be surprised should you find a complete absence of anything mystical or miraculous in the manifested reality of those who are so eager to advise you. Friends and family who suffer the lack of abundance, joy, love, fulfillment and prosperity in their own lives really have no business imposing their self-limiting beliefs on your reality experience."
— **Anthon St. Maarten**

Limiting beliefs are another threat to your confidence. They are often used as an excuse to avoid facing pain. Someone might think they aren't smart enough to pursue their career goals and give up without achieving anywhere near their actual potential.

I know a guy who as a child dreamed of becoming an astronaut. His father made fun of this dream and it left him discouraged. After university he worked for years at a small office that sells electric accessories. He hated it. He realized he still had that dream. He was worried he was too stupid to accomplish anything. Because that's what his father always told him. Determined to prove the old jerk wrong he went back to school to get a PHD in astronomy and physics. Now he works at a large observatory and is very happy to be doing something related to his passion.

Many people aren't even that fortuitous. When faced with rejection or criticism we hide from it. As we are afraid to take responsibility for the action we adopt convenient excuses to explain why we would never succeed anyway. For example, a short guy might have been rejected by a girl he had a crush on when he was younger. He wants to pretend he has no control over her reaction to him. So he places the blame on his height. He lies to himself that, "women ONLY date tall men." This deception allows him to feel slightly less pain. If he had to honestly admit it was his negativity, insecurity, and poor social skills that turned her off then he must face the pain of admitting he is flawed. By pretending he was only rejected because he isn't tall enough he can try to protect himself with this bullshit illusion.

He is so terrified of honestly facing those flaws that he avoids socializing with women. After all, they would just reject him for his lack of height. In his mind he's convinced himself that dating works like this:

Step 1: Tall man approaches cute girl, "Hi you are cute. I'm tall."
Step 2: Girl responds with a smile and says, "Oh my god you are so tall!
 Take me home and do whatever you want and let's get married!"

In this warped narrative there is no room for social skills, authenticity, confidence, a sense of humor, having your life together, having hobbies you are passionate about, having great friends, Success in your field and life, being comfortable being yourself, knowing how to lead and so on. In his mind none of that is important at all to building a connection with a girl. Even when girls like him he will still be looking for proof that they are rejecting him for not being tall enough. He cares more about defending this unsubstantiated excuse than actually finding a girlfriend.

What are the bullshit stories you tell yourself?

The socially anxious often create negative narratives to justify their inability to face their fears. Finish the following sentences to find what ridiculous stories you have been using to hold yourself back. Try to fill in the blanks for as many of these sentences as you can.

- When I meet new people I can't _____. (ex: be honest)
- On a date I can't _____ (ex: build trust, attraction)
- People never want to date me because _____.
- People never want to hang out with me because _____.
- People never_____ me. (ex: listen to, talk to, appreciate)
- People never _____ (ex: start conversations with me)
- When I talk to people I always feel _____ (ex: fake)
- People always think I'm_____ (ex: quiet, shy, stupid)
- People always _____ me. (ex: ignore, listen to)

- At work I can't _____. (ex: ask for help)
- If I tell a story people will _____ (ex: listen, be bored)
- If I try to start conversations people will react by _____ (ex: listening, ignoring, doing whatever they feel like)
- People never like that I _____

Pay extra attention to the sentences that include the words "always" and "never." It sounds extremely insecure to make an illogical statement like, "people never talk to me!" Really? Never? Not once in your life someone started a conversation with you? You've never had a conversation with another human being in your entire life? It's obviously complete bullshit. You could more accurately say, "Recently people don't often talk to me." But even that likely isn't true. If you tried you could find people willing to talk to you. But instead people hide behind these absolute statements in order to feel safe.

Anxiety sufferers are well practiced at tearing themselves down and horrible at being nice to themselves. Being kind to yourself is exactly what you need. If you can't be nice to yourself other people will be inclined to do the same.

Your mind will look for evidence to confirm whatever reality you pretend is real. If you pretend your looks or personality aren't good enough you'll constantly look for evidence to prove it.

There is a video you might have seen around the internet. Two teams are playing with a basketball. You are asked to count how many times the ball is passed. Most people focus on the ball. They never even realize a gorilla walked across the screen, beat its chest, and then walked off the screen while they were counting. When they watch the same video again they are surprised they missed it. You can only see what you looking for.

If you only look for evidence that you are unworthy of love, respect and attention that is exactly what you will find. These negative thoughts will make you feel like shit. And when you feel like shit, you will attract shitty experiences into your life. You will make people around you feel the same way. It's called state transference. Whatever state you feel influences how those around you feel. Fortunately, when you feel good you are more likely to encounter positive social interactions.

Social anxiety distorts your perception of yourself. You aren't necessarily too ugly, too short, or too boring. You have only led yourself to believe you have these negative qualities. Whatever you believe you will become. If you think you can't meet someone for friendship or more it's because you have already committed to anxiety and negative thoughts.

What are your limiting beliefs?
What do you believe is impossible for you?

These fears of inadequacy often start in childhood. They are the negative beliefs that accompany disowning parts of yourself. If a parent discourages you from pursuing a sport in school maybe you begin to believe you are weak and lack athleticism. This belief could prevent you from going to the gym to work on your physique. It could prevent you from seeing how athletic you actually have the potential to become.

These limiting beliefs can also come from the media. You may see images of people who are more successful, happier, and have better relationships than you and feel inadequate.

Open minded people are more willing to accept the truth even when it means accepting their own flaws and mistakes. This openness allows growth. Those suffering from severe limiting beliefs often refuse to caveat anything of these beliefs with "in general…" They wouldn't say, "In general women like tall guys." Instead they would say, "All women always only like tall guys," or "People never listen to me." They don't leave space for the possibility of exceptions or that they could be completely wrong. They speak with absolute certainty. It often seems they are more concerned with convincing themselves than other people.

When a limiting belief emerges it's your responsibility to confront it. Demand that limiting belief explain itself. If that belief is, "I'm not cool enough to talk to them," then imagine that belief as a person and stare into its lifeless eyes as you interrogate the poor bastard. What does it look like? Probably a weak, skinny, nerdy, fragile, loser with an ugly face but use your imagination.

Ask it, "Why aren't I cool enough?"

"Why are you trying to hold me back?"

"What painful truth are you trying to hide from me?"

Scare that limiting belief and get it to tell you everything it knows. Keep a record of recurring limiting beliefs. Be sure to note down what triggers them and make an effort to challenge them.

Acknowledge the pain or disowned part of yourself the limiting belief is meant to protect you from. Ask yourself, "Is there another way to see myself in this situation?" Be open to the possibility that you could be smart enough, interesting enough, or adequate enough to talk to people with authenticity and confidence.

If you have a limiting belief that making mistakes is bad you'll avoid many growth opportunities because you won't be willing to fail. It's a major reason people avoid learning new skills they are actually interested in.

For another example, the belief that rejection is bad could prevent you from approaching new people and you'll miss out on meeting a lot of great people and potential friends.

If you can change this belief to something more positive, rejection won't be as scary. You could see it as a learning experience. Every time a social interaction doesn't go well you have an opportunity to learn something.

You can also believe that it's better to be rejected than to have someone politely waste your time. You could also imagine that rejection is just a word that describes when 2 people met and just couldn't build a connection. It's completely natural. You don't have to build an authentic connection with each person.

These positive beliefs may at first seem incongruent for the socially anxious. That's why it's important to challenge your existing limiting beliefs and maintain an open mind to explore new possibilities. With time these limiting beliefs will lose their power to control your behavior.

Here are more specific tips on overcoming your limiting beliefs:

Step 1: Become aware of your limiting beliefs

One of the most effective ways of developing this awareness is to practice mediation. When the world distracts you it might not be as obvious how many negative thoughts pop into your consciousness. With meditation you pay attention to these thoughts as they emerge from your subconscious. When you realize it's a limiting belief you've made the first step in diminishing them.

Avoid making excuses to justify your limiting beliefs. Maybe you use the excuse that you never have enough money to accomplish something. Is that just the victim mentality, or do you have alternatives?

Step 2: Write down your limiting beliefs

Be brutally honest with yourself. This is required to accurately reflect on your blind spots and see what you have to learn. Ignoring these realizations would only be denial. If you worry someday someone would see these notes it's only more indication you would be writing this stuff down and thinking about it. Keep the notes for as long as you need them.

Step 3: Disassociate yourself from your beliefs. Especially the Limiting ones.

People assume they are their beliefs about themselves. But you are not your beliefs. You are the awareness observing the beliefs that occur in your mind. Beliefs can and do change all the time. Shy people become extremely confident all the time. Extroverts experience trauma and lose trust in others all the time.

Whatever belief you have can be changed if you are open minded to truth.

Problems occur when you aren't willing to accept any alternative beliefs. The quiet polite guy might see logically that women react well to being teased. But he can't get himself to do it because he's invested so much in his boring approval seeking identity.

He compliments everything and never risks saying anything that could offend in the slightest. His identity is wrapped up in being the nice guy that makes everyone feel good. His mind is closed to the possibility that this needy behavior can often make people uncomfortable. In fact if he could connect with his authenticity, develop a sense of humor and playfully joke around in conversation people would be much happier to interact with him.

Identifying with the mind and its limiting beliefs prevents realignment with your authenticity. Thinking you are your beliefs, especially the nasty, negative, limiting ones only alienates yourself from others and yourself. People who suffer from this alienation often have an emotionless stare in their eyes. They are absorbed in thought, often worry, and they don't see anything outside themselves.

Pay attention to people and you will clearly see the difference between those enjoying the present moment and those with a lifeless stare and zero emotion.

They aren't present.

Their mind is in the past or future.

Even when they talk to you they are worrying about what you think of them. They need to impress everyone so they put on a mask and try to win approval. The socially intelligent can clearly recognize this behavior as fake. The only people who might not are other fake people.

There are many suggested methods for disassociating from your limiting beliefs. Here we will discuss a few methods and you can choose several to try out.

Rephrase the belief

Instead of simply thinking the thought, rephrase it to show yourself you are aware of it. Such as instead of thinking, "I'm too fat to dance." Rephrase it in your mind to "*I am thinking that* I'm too fat to dance." In this way, it's not an absolute statement you are forcing yourself to believe. This way of phrasing makes you less anxious because you put less pressure on yourself to believe it.

Stop!

Every time you have a negative thought or limiting belief build a habit of telling yourself to stop! Then rephrase the statement to something more positive and helpful. Such as instead of thinking, "nobody here is talking to me," it could be more helpful to admit, "I'm not talking to anyone, and I want to go talk to someone." And then you go talk to someone.

The negative limiting belief implies you aren't worthy of talking to others. You are good enough, so go find someone worthy of conversation with you.

External Voice

Try this when you are particularly plagued with negative limiting thoughts. Imagine all those cruel thoughts about yourself aren't coming from your own mind. Imagine they are coming from someone following you around all day. How does it feel? Would you really allow someone to treat you like this? Likely not. So why belittle and ridicule yourself so much?

Is this thought helpful?

When you think of your limiting beliefs ask yourself if it is actually helping you. Instead of assuming your thoughts about not being interesting enough to start a conversation can't be changed, ask yourself what use these thoughts have at all. If anything they discourage you from socializing.

Step 4: Challenge the truth behind each belief

Interrogate your beliefs. Ask yourself:

Is this belief true?

When you ask this your gut instinct might be to shout "yes!" Because that is what you are used to doing. Your identity depends on maintaining this belief. Even the most compelling evidence might not persuade you to give it up because you are worried about losing yourself. You've invested too much in the belief and you are scared admitting you could have been wrong all along.

Imagine you are at a theme park and there is a ride you want to go on. It looks really fun to you so you get in line. It's actually a very long line. You wait about 15 minutes before you realize it might take 2 hours to get to the ride. You think about jumping out of the line, but decide to stay in it anyway. Well after you've been in the line 1 hour you realize it could take another 2 hours maybe even a little more before you can get to the ride! Would you stay in line? Just go to any major theme park such as Disney Land when it's busy for the answer. Most people stand in ridiculously long lines for 2 or more hours all the time!

Even when people debate running away to some shorter line they usually decide to stubbornly stay where they are.

Why?

Because they've already invested so much time in that line! If you only wasted 1 or 2 minutes in a line and then realize you could spend three hours waiting it's easier to decide to run away. You don't care about losing that brief moment. But if you already invested an hour in the line, you are much more likely stay put when you realize you could be waiting another 2 hours! This is because you feel like you would lose that 1 hour time you invested in line if you ran away now. Instead of admitting this was a poor choice of ride and finding something faster you decide to waste a total of 3 hours of your life instead of only 1!

This is the same with the limiting beliefs you've invested in. You've already spent so much time and energy investing in them it seems like a waste of your life if you admit they were the wrong choice.

You might be able to fool yourself that your limiting beliefs are helping you but they aren't. They just hold you back. Also they are completely obvious to socially intelligent people who see through the disgusting fakeness. It's not cool. So cut it out.

If you still aren't convinced about the invalidity of a limiting belief then ask some harder questions:

Has anyone ever proven this belief wrong?

What exceptions to this belief are there?

How does this belief make you feel?

How would you feel if you were forced to confront evidence disproving this belief?

And here is the most important question: Who would you be without that limiting belief?

You might feel different without that belief. But it should be liberating, not frightening. Think about how your life would be different without that belief. Think about how your life will continue to be more of the same if you never change it. Visualize a life without this limiting belief. When you finally let go of the resistance you will likely see the benefits of being more open minded with your beliefs.

Chapter 9: Giving Versus Taking

"Why is true success so relatively effortless? It might be likened to the magnetic field created by an electric current running through a wire. The higher the power of the current, the greater the magnetic field that it generates. And the magnetic field itself then influences everything in its presence. There are very few at the top. The world of the mediocre, however, is one of intense competition, and the bottom of the pyramid is crowded. Charismatic winners are sought out; losers have to strive to be accepted. People who are loving, kind, and thoughtful of others have more friends than they can count; success in every area of life is a reflex to those who are aligned with successful patterns. And the capacity to be able to discern the difference between the strong patterns of success and the weak patterns leading to failure is now available to each of us."
— **David R. Hawkins, Power vs. Force**

You can only be rejected if you are trying to take something. When you are giving without expecting anything in return there is nothing to reject.

You can demonstrate this to yourself with an experiment. Don't just imagine it. Actually take 10 minutes of your day and go do it because it's both easy and profound.

Step 1: In a public area outside ask random people for a quarter, a euro, or a small unit of whatever the local currency is.

Before and during each approach pay attention to how you feel. What does it feel like?

Step 2: This time you need to give the money away. Use the coins you got in step 1 if you received any.

How did you feel this time? You will likely realize that when you are trying to take value from others you feel a lot more nervous. However when you try to give money away for free it felt a lot easier. Some people might not accept the gift of your few coins if they assume it's a conditional gift.

It doesn't matter.

The point is that when you talk to people with the intention of sharing value, such as happiness, love, your sense of humor, advice or anything it helps you connect to your authenticity and relax in the moment. However, when you have an agenda you are attached to the outcome of the interaction. This attachment not only sabotages your positive emotions, it also ruins your results.

When you feel you are incomplete you act as if you need something from others to survive. Your expressions, body language, and tone of voice will shout neediness. It is the definition of creepy. People feel the needy vibe and impulsively reject your attempt to take value away from them.

When a smelly beggar suddenly pokes you and demands change what's your immediate reaction? Do you feel compassion for your fellow human being and automatically smile? Do you reach into your deep pockets to pull out a handful of coins to share? Maybe some people are that generous. But we know even the kindest person may react by instinctively putting distance between themselves and the beggar.

If you feel you aren't good enough you are like that smelly beggar. You reek of approval seeking and will push away even the nicest people. The only people who will be willing to hang out with you will be other beggars. Together you will complain about how it's so unfair people with money and clean clothes get all the attention from attractive, successful people.

If only they could love you for who you are. You may give compliments in the hope of winning the affection or pocket change of a beautiful stranger. But it will be so obvious that you are a beggar that rejection is inevitable. In fact she doesn't need to reject you. You've already rejected yourself.

Taking comes from a very needy place. People sometimes do manage to develop social skills despite neediness and disowned pain hiding inside them. But these skills are like a shiny veneer painted around an outhouse. Sure it might look cool from the outside, but get close and look inside. It will still smell like an outhouse.

When you are taking you feel you need these tricks and lies to manipulate people into giving you what you want. A businessman may not be forthcoming about all the dangers of his product. A woman may pretend she's only slept with a third of the men she's actually been with to impress a man she'd like to settle down with. When you deceive in these ways you put even more pressure on yourself to succeed.

Your neediness and negativity increase. Instinctually we have a desire to be social and build connection. But if you feel the need to do this through deception and manipulation this inconsistency will manifest as awkwardness, incongruence, and fear.

If however you come from the frame that you are already complete then there is nothing you need from other people. You won't be needy, therefore you can't be rejected. There is nothing to reject. You aren't attached to the approval or value you could get from another person if you take the giving perspective.

When you already know you are enough you don't need validation, attention, or value from others. If someone doesn't want to talk to you it doesn't matter. You didn't need their attention. Your emotions remain the same because you likely didn't even see it as rejection no matter how antisocial someone actually was. If someone doesn't want to socialize with you it's their loss. This shouldn't be seen as arrogant if you actually are just giving happiness away for free.

If someone isn't interested in talking to you there will always be other people happy to share whatever you offer. When you don't need anything outside you to feel good you won't need people to give you positive reactions. You won't need to give up control of your emotions to external forces.

From the taking perspective other people hold all the value. The taker sees other people as holding pieces of candy while he has none. To get the candy he feels the need to lie about who he is since he believes he isn't good enough for a piece of candy as himself.

He'll pretend, "I have a million dollars and I drive an expensive Ferrari, look this is the key to it!" in the hopes this false front will be attractive enough to deserve the candy. The whole time he will stink of neediness.

The giver doesn't need to manipulate. In fact he has so much candy he can't finish it. He is willing to give it away for free to anyone. Even to the taker who thinks he needs to lie to get it! Now doesn't the taker look even more ridiculous? The taker has nothing of value to offer. At least, he believes so. If only he would look inside and realize he has so much more to share. The giver doesn't mind when people don't want a piece of the candy. The candy still has value and he can give it to someone else or even enjoy it himself. Rejection doesn't exist in the giver's world.

The world is always changing. If you depend on it for your emotional state it's like jumping into a cage with a hungry tiger and begging it not to eat you. Sure the tiger might be friendly to people and not see you as food. But for how long? Eventually you might regret that choice.

You can't control everything that happens in the world. Social leeches try to control the world and the results they get from it. They think that by taking value they can finally get the happiness they crave. You don't really want badass social skills or confidence. Those come easily enough when you are happy anyway. What you really want to is that internally validated sense of joy. The giver already has that joy because he accepts reality however it is. He doesn't depend on external reality for his happiness.

To eliminate the taker mentality recognize that you don't need anything from anyone. When you talk to people give your full attention, emotions, and honestly share yourself without needing anything in return.

Chapter 10: Achieving your Social Confidence Goals

"The only thing standing between you and your goal is the bullshit story you keep telling yourself as to why you can't achieve it."

— Jordon Belfort

If you could suddenly be as confident as you hope how would your life be different?

What kinds of people would you want in your life?

What activities would you finally feel comfortable doing?

What new career opportunities would be available to you?

What new skills could you finally learn?

What new places could you finally go?

What social events will you finally be able to attend and enjoy?

In what ways would your life be better?

Thinking and writing about the answers to these questions gives you a look at what's really important to you.

These are the things you actually want in your life. Fear is often used as an excuse to avoid realizing your own potential.

Goals usually represent your values. This means if you value friendship and humor your goal might be to meet new people and share fun conversation with them. The fear of being judged might prevent you from doing this. If you value creativity your goal might be to create something beautiful for people to enjoy. And again the fear of people judging your art will prevent you from taking action or at least prevent you from taking risks you are interested in exploring.

When you have goals that you care about but let fear get in the way you often end up making yourself feel worse. Because your actions (avoidant behavior) are inconsistent with your values (making friends, pursuing exciting career options, group activities etc.) Some people remain stuck in boring jobs they hate not only for the security of a consistent paycheck but because of all the social awkwardness they could encounter if they tried to find a new job. Going to job interviews, networking, meeting new coworkers, the new boss having a bad attitude and more. All these worrisome thoughts trigger avoidant behavior. These individuals will convince themselves it's safer to keep flipping burgers instead of applying for a job or attending classes related to something they actually care about.

Avoiding social situations required to get what you really care about in life is completely incongruent. It will make you very dissatisfied with life. To examine how much more satisfied you could be imagine meeting the ideal version of yourself from 20 years in the future. This version of you has conquered their fears.

What amazing adventures and experiences have they had that you feel incapable of?

What fears did they face?

What places did they go to?

What accomplishments have they enjoyed?

What skills did they learn?

How are their relationships with family and friends?

How is their life different from where your life is heading now?

Honestly answer these questions. It will be helpful to write them down in your progress journal and really visualize how your life could be different if every time you are tempted to avoid authentic social interaction you actually took action to achieve the goals you care about.

Don't let negative thoughts impede your imagination. Assume you have plenty of money, time, and good health to accomplish all of these. This vision of your life may be vastly different from what your actions would indicate.

What are your values and goals?

Social conditioning shouldn't control your values. Don't worry if your values and goals are different from other people. This is about you and what you truly want from life.

Instead of saying, "My goal is to start conversations without feeling nervous" It's better to say, "My goal is to start conversations."

If you feel nervous it should be acceptable. That nervous feeling is an indication of something in your subconscious that should be addressed. If you value socializing, making friends, and relationships then starting conversations should count as a success no matter how you are feeling when you do it!

What values are important to you in relationships?

Some examples are sense of humor, authenticity, trust, ambition, compassion, spontaneity, dependability, open-mindedness, and intelligence.

Write down your values and figure out what you want from relationships with others. For each of your values think of situations where it's difficult for you to express this value yourself. Such as if you value humor but sometimes are afraid to say something humorous to people you have just met.

Or if you value authenticity but have trouble sharing your real opinions. Once you have established your values the goals should become obvious.

If you really care about making connections with other people you should have many goals related to social interactions. Such as maintaining eye contact, speaking loudly, being able to share your opinions, or changing any behaviors which inhibit you in social situations.

By now you should have written down your values and goals. The more invested you are in avoidant behavior the more difficult it will be to acknowledge what you really care about.

If you have read up to this point you should be willing to honestly explore what you want from life.

Having goals is great. It puts you in a positive mood. Unfortunately it's not enough. Next you need a plan and you need to take action. If you need help with goal setting check out another book of mine, <u>Goal Setting: The Proven Plan to Achieve Personal and Career Goals.</u>

If you want to get good at talking with people, fun conversation, and confidently expressing yourself in social situations you need to talk to lots of people.

Find some social events you can attend. You could start greeting people you meet during the day. As you practice, you'll be able to comfortably have longer conversations.

Whatever social situation you fear, make a plan to face that fear.

If you are afraid of casual conversation with strangers, start at least one random conversation every day.

If you are afraid of talking on the telephone you can make a few phone calls to old friends and if you are scared to answer the phone remind yourself you want to overcome this irrational fear.

If you are afraid of what people think of you, practice complaining. If food in the restaurant has a problem feel free to tell the waiter. If someone is behaving rudely, calmly, with a loud voice tell them their behavior is inappropriate.

If you are afraid of sharing your opinion or personal information it's time you finally start practicing honesty with others.

If you are afraid of asking for help ask a few random people for directions. You can also ask coworkers or teachers for help when you need it.

If you are afraid of people watching you, then you can wait in line at a coffee shop or similar establishment and when it's your turn, take your time and order very slowly. Don't let the tension of people waiting behind you bother you. Go to crowded places. If you really aren't sure if you are doing some action correctly, it's perfectly acceptable to ask someone if your technique is correct.

If you are afraid of public speaking you can likely find opportunities to practice this skill. There are many clubs, and organizations that would require you to speak in front of others. You can also attend free lectures you are interested in at universities and ask questions.

Whatever social situation you fear, you can think of the solution to curing it.

For each of these fears you likely anticipate a negative outcome you'd like to avoid. For example, you may be afraid of starting conversations with strangers. You might worry someone will be rude to you or not interested in talking with you. Depending on how you approach, many people are at least open to giving you a chance. Even if they are rude in response to your friendliness so what?

You didn't die.

You are fine.

Logically you get this. But you still have that negative emotional reaction trying to pull you away from starting the conversation. Don't resist those feelings. Sit with them. Accept them. Before entering social situations that scare you visualize the situation clearly. Imagine all your words and actions.

Then imagine everything going horribly wrong.

All your worst fears have happened.

If your core fear is worry people will judge you for stuttering when you are nervous, then imagine that is exactly what happens. Turn up the visual clarity in your imagination 1000% Imagine You've just started a conversation and feel nervous. You try to speak but you can barely get anything out.

You feel everyone's looks of disgust glued onto your every action as they laugh and mock you. Over exaggerate the worst possible outcome in this way.

Even though it isn't real, most people feel some discomfort in this exercise.

Next, you must accept both this undesirable outcome, and your feelings about it. Look at each embarrassing detail and allow it to exist.

Look inside at your emotional reaction and accept it in the same ways we have discussed throughout this book.

By accepting your core fear, such as being judged, rejected, socially inadequate etc. you can make progress in overcoming these inhibitions. If for example someone refused to accept

This is most effective before and during an event you usually associate with anxiety. However you can still use it when you are alone and want to work on it with your imagination.

For each of your fears imagine the worst case scenario.

Practice accepting whatever feelings and thoughts emerge no matter how uncomfortable.

Chapter 11: Rejection

"Adapt what is useful, reject what is useless, and add what is specifically your own."
— Bruce Lee

You can't say yes to every opportunity that comes into your life. You will inevitably choose to invest in certain people, careers, and activities. This requires rejecting the alternatives. Since you are allowed to reject things you don't want in your life, it should be acceptable for people to reject you too. Can you imagine if we lived by a moral obligation to never reject anyone for any reason? That means all the nasty people who wanted to could insert themselves into your life and there would be nothing you could do about it. You would have to date them, wash their disgusting backs, and worse.

Unfortunately, many people don't care enough about their own standards to reject things they don't actually want. They end up in careers and relationships they aren't actually satisfied with. In their attempt to satisfy everyone they end up living a lie that inevitably disappoints everyone involved.

People who don't know how to reject others are often the same people who don't take rejection well.

Fear of rejection is learned from experiences viewed as more traumatizing than they need to be. Maybe as a child a man's crush said she didn't want to talk to him again, so he let that pain prevent him from talking to another girl again. In response he creates an imaginary vision of reality in which he isn't good enough for any woman.

As a result he gravitates towards people with similar thoughts. Together they complain that all women are superficial bitches who would never be interested in men like them. Whenever they encounter people with completely opposite views of reality they ignore it. They actively seek out other people who confirm their warped sense of reality. And in this reality rejection has become a negative, terrifying part of life that prevents him from actually experiencing a real human connection.

People addicted to their negative thoughts can't stand to be around positive high energy people. If the negative person complains they don't get the reinforcement that their victim mentality is correct. Instead they will complain, but the positive person doesn't make an effort to reinforce their bullshit.

You see this all the time among negative people. They moan about how the world just isn't fair. And then their buddies, or any other negative people will confirm their suspicions that greedy, superficial people are conspiring to ruin their life.

If you try to explain to people lost in the putrid haze of negativity that it's their mindset and not their physical appearance that is keeping them single they will refuse to accept it no matter what evidence you present them.

You could share stories of people facing rejection, developing social skills and real inner confidence and it just doesn't resonate with them. You could show them proven paths to overcoming their insecurities and they would refuse to look. They are too invested in their negativity and the false assumption that rejection is equal to death. In truth, the more you have been rejected the more you can live.

If you are on the fence between viewing rejections as the benign inevitability they actually are and as a scary force to be avoided at all costs I strongly urge you to take at least half a step out of your comfort zone. You will see that "rejection" is just a word. The negativity associated with it only exists in your mind.

Rejection is inevitable. Accept rejection instead of hiding from it. Avoiding rejection only makes things worse.

If you are scared of rejection the best choice you can make is to spend a period of time training yourself to seek out and accept rejection. It will feel uncomfortable. Accept it. People won't want to fulfill your requests. Accept it. You will grow the guts to reject people and situations you absolutely don't want in your life. You will also have the courage to take a risk when it's important to you.

Rejection therapy

Exposure is used to treat issues such as OCD, phobias, and social anxiety. When you expose yourself to your fear you can't stay scared forever.

To start accepting rejection as the normal part of life it is and not the traumatic experience the socially anxious over exaggerate it to be you simply need to make requests and not worry about the result.

For a period of at least 10 days aim to get rejected at least once a day. Quite a few people have turned their lives around with this method.

In his book Rejection Proof, author Jia Jiang explains what he learned from 100 days of consecutive exposure to rejection. He got so sick of fear and his needy mindset that he decided to desensitize himself to the pain of rejection. Before this shy guy embarked on this challenge rejections always devastated him. He forced himself to view every rejection as a success.

He turned this into a game and although it started awkwardly he quickly associated positive feelings with overcoming these social anxieties and his fear of rejection.

By turning rejection into the goal previously awkward situations were no longer painful.

The first day he tried to borrow $100 from a security guard. As he approached he wondered how he would be rejected.

"Would he cuss me out? Laugh at me? Whip out his nightstick and start clubbing me? Would he think I was a nutcase and call me the nearest mental hospital asking if any Asian male patient had gone missing while holding me in a headlock?"

Finally he approached and asked to borrow the money. The security guard simply frowned and replied, "No. why?" He replied "all right. Thanks," and quickly ran away as he was still feeling that rush of fear. He reviewed the video and realized that the security guard was willing to extend the conversation but instead Jia let fear turn him into a *"bumbling idiot."*

The next day he asked for a "burger refill" at a restaurant when he noticed they had a sign that said Free Refill, obviously referring to drinks. Later he reviewed the video of this conversation and realized even though he was clearly a bit nervous, he was capable of asking a follow up question to keep the awkward conversation going. He didn't let rejection bother him. The employee didn't seem bothered and in fact was smiling and found the request humorous. In fact most people he interacted with had similar responses.

On the third day he walked into a Krispy Kreme donut shop and asked for specialized donuts in the shape of the Olympic rings and he needed it within 15 minutes. Surprisingly the donut artist fulfilled this request at no charge after a friendly conversation.

You never know what is possible if you never try. Jia continued this experiment for a total of 100 days.

Along the way he internalized many lessons. Not only about accepting rejection but also about how to improve the likelihood of getting the results you want in social interactions.

He claims he did this to more fearlessly take on entrepreneurial challenges. But the lessons he learned are important for anyone who fears rejection.

He learned to accept his anxious feelings and as a result he was no longer afraid.

Jia's other rejection challenges included:

- Asking to deliver a pizza for dominos
- Send something to Santa Claus through Fed Ex
- Ask a stranger for a compliment
- Challenge a CEO to a staring contest
- Plant a flower in someone's yard
- Exchange secrets with a stranger
- Take a picture with a stranger
- Play soccer in someone's backyard
- Be a live mannequin at Abercrombie
- Be a greeter at Starbucks
- Make a sale for BestBuy
- Ask for a free room at a hotel
- Ask for a bike race at Toys R Us
- Ask waitress for a dance
- Sell cookies for the girl scouts
- Ask strangers to rate your look
- Ask to borrow book at Barnes & Noble
- Rock paper scissors with a stranger
- Ask for a discount at Target

Hopefully you can think of some of your own challenges. You just need to make a request that is outside of your comfort zone. You can start with requests that are easy.

Gradually increase the ridiculousness and difficulty of each request. Very socially anxious people may have trouble making even simple requests. Don't be ashamed if you have to start with something you think wouldn't bother most people.

Here are some possible requests:

- Ask for directions
- Ask for help carrying something
- Ask someone for a breath mint, or piece of gum
- Challenge stranger to arm wrestle. (This one is fun)
- Ask someone if they like your shoes
- Ask someone to sing for you
- Go to a fast food restaurant and ask a stranger for a French Fry
- Ask someone if they can tell you a good joke
- Ask someone to listen to you tell a joke and judge your delivery
- Ask someone if they think your voice sounds ok.
- In a public sitting area, ask someone to give you their seat.

- Ask someone if they'd like a free haircut.
- Ask someone to tie your shoes for you.
- Learn a magic trick and ask strangers if you can demonstrate it for them. (Depending on the energy you give off people won't likely reject this request because you are offering to give value instead of taking it.)
- Ask a stranger to judge a drawing you made in 2 minutes.
- Hold a free hugs sign and try to hug strangers (or do this without the sign.)

Rejection therapy reverses the impact of years of accumulated avoidant behavior. In small increments fear can be neutralized. But it requires action.

When you invest in fearful avoidance it squeezes your comfort zone into a tight noose around your neck. Remember, rejection won't ruin your life. But *fear* of rejection might.

100 intentional days of rejection probably seems like a huge commitment most people aren't willing to make.

Life will get in the way and eventually you'll be back to old habits before finishing so why even start anyway?

It should however be reasonable for anyone to commit to 10 consecutive days of rejection therapy to see the results for themselves. If the mind blowing epiphanies aren't enough by then continue for 30 days or longer.

The first attempt is often the hardest. Walking up to a stranger will trigger anxiety and risk avoidance. The more severe your social anxiety the more stress hormones your brain will produce to cope with the imagined danger. You'll spit out your requests and inside you'll feel scared. But external reality will be completely safe. You'll have no choice but to confront the only reasonable conclusion, *"oh... That actually wasn't so bad."*

Consistency is important. For the next 10 days or more look for opportunities to practice rejection therapy daily.

Rules of the 10 Day Rejection Therapy Challenge:

1. You must get rejected at least once a day.
2. If you aren't rejected during a day it doesn't count and you should start over at day 1.
3. You must be out of your comfort zone and feeling vulnerable. It can't be easy for you.
4. It only counts if your request is denied.

You should feel uncomfortable but you shouldn't intentionally make people offended or angry. If you aren't getting rejected then you likely haven't yet stepped out of your comfort zone.

You will eventually see there is no reason to get upset about these perceived rejections. With enough experience you will realize that rejection doesn't change anything about you. You are still the same person. People who do face their social fears live more fulfilled lives because their comfort zones are vast. They attract more opportunities into their reality.

The fight or flight response diminishes with each request. It no longer needs to protect your precious ego because you will be more internally validated in social interaction. The more you experience fear and shame the more they decrease. They can't kill you anyway. You won't completely diminish these instinctual responses. But you can learn how to live with them.

After you go through this period you will feel an immense relief. As if you've finally learned how to be human. There will however still be times when a request you would like to make triggers that fearful urge to avoid.

These will be crucial moments where you need to decide if you actually want to invest in a more fearless and happy version of yourself or if you want to return to the irrational fears of your past.

There is nothing wrong with rejection. People are allowed to decide they don't want to interact with you. They may be completely wrong. But they are free to make mistakes too. Everyone is obsessed with thinking about themselves. Nobody will even remember your odd requests.

This challenge is an investment in your freedom to express yourself confidently. If you really want confidence you owe it to yourself to give it a try.

The only question is, when will you start?

Once you've chosen the start date plan out 10 requests of increasing difficulty.

The first one should be something you are sure you could accomplish. Such as asking someone if they can give you a piece of gum. The tenth request should be very challenging for you.

As you get increasingly out of your comfort zone remind yourself to accept the anxious feelings while you are doing the request. See how long you can stretch out the interaction. Don't run away from fear. Embrace it.

After 10 days of general Rejection Therapy. It's time to apply the lessons you internalized to things you actually care about.

Now you must do the same challenge for at least 3 things you ACTUALLY want within a week.

Examples:

- Ask for a date with someone you find attractive
- Start a conversation with attractive strangers you would actually like to get to know.
- Apply to a job you really want but might not be qualified for
- If you worry about your looks, ask people if they think you are good looking. Their opinion is only subjective, it's not fact. So just accept the reality that they are entitled to their opinions and you are entitled to yours. To be blunt, no matter how you look, it's usually the negative low self-esteem people who will try to insult you anyway. If they see a chance to tear down someone's confidence they often take it.
- Ask people about your appearance, face, clothes or some other quality about yourself you are insecure about. While you might hope to receive some compliments here, accept the fact you don't need those kind words to feel good about yourself.
- Ask boss for a 3 week vacation when the company usually only allows 2 weeks off.

- Ask to borrow money from a friend or family member if you actually need it.
- Ask for a favor you really need
- Ask for help
- Apply for a selective class, conference, or activity you would like to join

You know what you care about. After 10 days of accepting rejection for odd requests in which you might not actually care about the results it's time to intentionally risk rejection for some things that actually matter to you. Choose as at least 3 of your own that really matter to you. You can make these 3 requests in a single day if you can. But don't wait more than a week to complete them all.

This will be a little different because you likely feel more attachment to getting a date from someone you are interested in as opposed to asking to borrow a dollar from a stranger. You didn't need that dollar. But somehow you might have convinced yourself you need the affection of someone you are interested in even more. In truth, you don't *need* either.

Attachment to results makes you a prisoner. Accepting the outcome allows you to be at peace with reality. You no longer need to resist because there is nothing to resist. Author of *The Success Principles,* Jack Canfield urges people to *"live with high intention and low attachment."* This means take action to get what you want but don't require any certain result. Attachment to the results you want leaves you bitter and disappointed. It makes you waste energy on negativity, fear and avoidance. If you accept whatever results you receive it frees you to explore more options.

Outcome dependency is a major cause of social anxiety. When you are attached to getting what you want from a social interaction it drains your energy.

Your mind starts wasting energy on strategies to get the result you want. Maybe you hope the other person will smile, ask you questions, like you, love you, date you, compliment you, or at least have a fun conversation with you. Maybe you want your colleagues to think you are cool. Maybe you want that girl to think you are funny so you say some awkward lines you've heard your friends use before in the hopes of getting the same results they did.

Ironically these schemes are more likely to harm your results instead of help them. They not only drain your energy but socially intelligent people see right through them. The more attached to a result you are the worse you will feel.

People with the most outcome dependency are the most negative and insecure. They have more to lose from social situations because their happiness, self-esteem and self-worth all come from the attention they receive from others. If someone were to reject their request it would mean they are unlovable and would destroy their emotional state.

When you can approach people without needing a result you are actually more likely to receive the result you want. Nervous feelings won't interfere with your ability to persuade others. When you can finally approach people without feeling the need to impress them to get what you want you will finally be able to express yourself confidently. In the next chapter we will discuss how to apply the same concepts to even more high pressure social situations.

Chapter 12: How to Be Assertive

Our ultimate freedom is the right and power to decide how anybody or anything outside ourselves will affect us."
— Stephen R. Covey

An exaggerated need for social approval is your largest obstacle to mastering social confidence. When you care too much what people think of you it can be devastating to realize you won't be loved by everyone no matter how legendary you are.

Not caring what people think of you doesn't mean you'll automatically become a narcissistic psychopath. You can still accept critical feedback and use this information to adjust your behavior if necessary. You can still care what people think of you to the extent it allows you to be a functioning member of society. However we all know this desire for social acceptance can overpower your ability to express yourself authentically.

To break free from an unhealthy addiction to social approval, there are three vital steps:

1. Develop internal validation
2. Practice accepting rejection even for things you care about
3. Practice assertiveness. Especially when it matters to you.

Previous chapters of this book have provided multiple methods and ideas to help you develop internal validation. By balancing unbalanced emotions, reintegrating disowned parts of yourself into your personality, and letting go of negative emotional states you will begin to accept yourself. With acceptance comes self-compassion and a reduced dependence on other people for positive emotions.

When you go inside yourself for internal validation, you no longer need the newest smart phone, coolest clothes, most interesting job, or hottest girlfriend to feel happy. Those external things can give you a glimpse of pleasure, but you'll constantly be chasing happiness. And remember, chasing happiness only reinforces your belief that you aren't happy.
Fear of rejection comes from needing people to approve of you and everything associated with you.

People think they need the coolest clothes and careers to impress others. If you ask men why they want a hot girlfriend, many insecure guys will admit it's because impressing their friends is more important to them than the biological instinct to find the perfect mate. In fact, it often seems the more insecure a guy is the more likely he will be to choose a girlfriend based on her ability to make his buddies jealous. Before he's had a single conversation with her he's already decided she is good enough to be his girlfriend and maybe more. He has no idea what his life would be like with her. He only cares about winning the social approval of others who see him with this attractive woman. Of course this equally applies to insecure women too.

The highly insecure guy isn't complete. He has a hole inside and he wants other people to fill it. When he sees the stunningly beautiful girl he is instantly attached to the outcome of getting a relationship with her. As he approaches he fantasizes about dating her, taking a picture and then posting it on Facebook to see how many "Likes" he gets. If he had to choose between dating her secretly in order to be intimate, or dating her openly but with no physical intimacy, he'd choose to make sure everyone knows he's dating her knowing he'd never actually be able to touch her.

As his attachment to getting a smile, conversation, phone number, a date and then a relationship from her is so immense, consequently so too is his fear of rejection at every step of the process.

It's like he is tiptoeing through a rejection mine field. Any misstep could obliterate his fragile ego. But the truth is it's not a mine field. It's a beautiful beach. The internally validated individual will stroll through the interaction with little problem. He might step on a jelly fish once in a while but it won't kill his opinion of himself.

Imagine going to a beach with your friends. Everyone is having fun. But then some weirdo comes along and is terrified there are bombs buried in the sand that will kill him. Not as a joke and there is no reason he should have this irrational belief. Wouldn't you think something is wrong with this guy?

By taking the steps to develop internal validation you no longer need to be that weirdo battling through a hallucinated haze of danger. You can start accepting rejection as the inevitability it is without it blowing up in your face.

The next step is to practice assertiveness. When we accept rejection we accept the reality that not everyone is willing to provide for us or allow us into their lives. When we practice assertiveness we take this a step further by intentionally making statements we know contain a certain degree of risk.

The truth is, you owe it not only to yourself but to everyone to be as authentic as possible. Approval motivated self-censorship makes us boring and dull.

It is tempting to think conformity will cause others to love us. But they don't really love *you* as a unique individual. They don't even know who you are if you've never really asserted your individuality.

However, when you can assertively express yourself, people will recognize this and love you for it.

Some people won't like you. But so what? At least some people will genuinely love and understand the real you.

Which do you prefer, being tolerated by many, or genuinely loved by a few amazing people? The choice is easy. And statistically speaking, you are likely to have a lot of people loving you when you can finally express yourself authentically.

Assertiveness means you are able to articulate your desires and needs, and also that you are willing to listen to the wants and needs to others.

Randy Patterson, clinical psychologist and author of The Assertiveness Workbook: How to Express your Ideas and Stand Up for Yourself and Work and in Relationships says:

"In the passive style, all the world is allowed on stage but for you — your role is to be the audience and supporter for everyone else. In the aggressive style, you're allowed on stage but you spend most of your time shoving the others off, like in a lifelong sumo match. With the assertive style, everyone is welcome onstage. You are entitled to be a full person, including your uniqueness, and so are others."

Assertiveness doesn't mean you aggressively demand everything you desire. It simply means you recognize that everyone's point of view and desires are valid, including your own.

Assertiveness means that when you are upset with someone you are able to express your disagreement as calmly as possible. You are simply expressing your views, not demanding they be seen as objective truth.

Passive people may hide their hurt feelings and let these situations diminish their self-esteem and increase stress. Aggressive people might shout and encounter repercussions for not being able to control their anger, such as losing a job, getting arrested, or getting into a physical fight. Passive-aggressive people might just ignore or avoid the people who have offended them while the offending party remains completely oblivious.

Being assertive means you can usually express yourself appropriately to the situation. You don't need to get aggressive and you don't need to be passive.

Calm assertiveness is not our natural response to stressful situations. Usually, the flight or fight response inclines you to either avoid a situation, or aggressively push back against it. So it can take conscious effort to train yourself to react assertively.

Being silent about your wants in needs will just turn you into a push over. You will get taken advantage of and no one will even know it upsets you.

Some people even get used to a passive personality and assume no one will even listen to them if they try.

Perhaps sometimes they did try to assert themselves, but the memory of being rejected and ignored is strong. These memories remind them it isn't a good idea to be assertive.

But that belief is just a habit and can be changed.

By becoming aware of your beliefs, they can be edited. The fear of conflict, change and disapproval is a fear you will need to face if you really want confidence.

Assertiveness is a skill you should develop.

You don't need to assault people to get your opinion across.

You also don't need to hide your feelings. You can intelligently and calmly state exactly what you think and people can respect you for it.

As Patterson writes in his Assertiveness Workbook:

"Through assertiveness we develop contact with ourselves and with others. We become real human

beings with real ideas, real differences...and real flaws. And we admit all of these things. We don't try to become someone else's mirror. We don't try to suppress someone else's uniqueness. We don't try to pretend that we're perfect. We become ourselves. We allow ourselves to be there."

If you want to be real, and not just a copy of the interchangeable clones around you, then assertiveness is essential.

Here are a few tips for developing assertiveness:

1. **Learn to say NO.** People worry saying no implies they are selfish and inconsiderate to the needs of others. Saying no is healthy because it allows you to place limits on yourself and relationships. You don't develop any resentment for doing things you don't actually want to do. You also get respect for expressing what you really think.

2. **Practice making requests.** Lack of assertiveness is often just a habit. You are used to doing what people tell you to do. So start with small requests. Ask for a different seat when you go to a restaurant, ask people for small favors, like to pass a napkin or help with

a project.

3. **Let go of guilt.** If you are used to being a people pleaser guilt may prevent you from progressing. But giving up guilt is essential to becoming assertive. You don't need to feel like you are a bad person if you don't work extra hours for your boss or loan your friend money. If you don't want to do these things then you don't need to. Assert your desires without guilt. Remind yourself that you deserve respect and to be listened to.

4. **Express your needs, desires and feelings.** People don't automatically know what you need. Passive people often hope their needs will somehow be obvious. However, if you don't tell anyone, they will often be completely oblivious to your situation. If you really want people to be more considerate of your needs you need to be considerate of your own need to be understood, and respected.

Let people know exactly what you need. It's more helpful to tell your partner you'd like them to clean up because you are too busy to do it, than to criticize them for being lazy and messy. Assertiveness is clearly a vital skill in developing social confidence. When you encounter crucial moments in which you can choose between asserting your authentic reality and hiding your real thoughts you now know what to do.

Chapter 13: Self Amusement

"People rarely succeed unless they have fun in what they are doing."
— **Dale Carnegie**

Fear of rejection and abandonment hold back the socially anxious from expressing themselves. When they finally start handling their inner demons, facing potential rejection and accepting the reactions of others without attachment to any outcome it should be liberating. By using the methods and concepts discussed in this book it is possible to gradually free yourself from that haze of social fear. Unfortunately, if you've spent your life avoiding social situations this newfound freedom may be overwhelming at first.

If you actually follow through with the advice of this book you will eventually realize a creative freedom to mold social situations with your intent. Instead of being a silent observer of conversations you will start contributing your own thoughts, opinions, and authenticity.

This is the stage where instead of dreading social situations you finally start enjoying them without fear. This is a crucial opportunity to start practicing self-amusement.

This means instead of saying or doing things to win the admiration of others, you do them because you actually find it entertaining. It means you say something humorous and you don't check everyone's faces to make sure they approve. Self-amusement means you can make yourself laugh and you don't need everyone else to laugh with you.

This only happens when you have no ulterior motives. You sit with the moment and don't need anything from it. Self-amusement can be talking about any topic you are interested. It could be intellectual, political, controversial, boring or even a bit crazy and socially unacceptable.

However don't do crazy actions just to get people to pay attention to you. Self-amusement doesn't mean you need to be a clown. When you are relaxed and chatting with your friends, or playing a game with them that is a subtle example of self-amusement. You aren't seeking their reaction. You are just enjoying the moment.

You can approach every interaction with the mindset of, "How can I make this fun for myself?"

Even if you feel good by having boring conversation that is acceptable too because you are enjoying it. Your emotional state comes from your own actions. If you aren't having fun you can only blame yourself.

How to Self-Amuse

1. Accept your emotional state. Remember the meditation and introspection methods we've discussed in this book can help you develop a habit of accepting your feelings.

    People are sometimes embarrassed of their bad moods. They pretend to be happier and higher energy than they really are because they hope this act will fool others into liking them. But this mask of false positivity is completely transparent. On the other side they can see a face failing to hide the pain. If you do this, you aren't fooling anyone.

2. Step out of your comfort zone. Depending on how stifled you allowed yourself to become your mind might still be functioning on avoidance autopilot. If you've been practicing the methods in this book you will finally start thinking of things of ways to amuse yourself in interactions but the urge to resist will pop up,

as that may be your usual habit. These are crucial moments where you need to step out of your comfort zone and impact reality.

If you are so stuck in your head and worried about how others see you then you must do something different from your usual routine. Take baby steps if you must.

If you are used to passively listening to what others are saying, intentionally ask more questions. If that is too normal for you then start asking more interesting questions you find entertaining. Such as, "what's super power would you want?" or "What super hero would you want to date?" These are just examples. You should think of your own ways to amuse yourself in social interactions.

3. Test the limits of your comfort zone. After you start enjoying the moment, making silly statements, asking fun questions you will finally start feeling socially confident. It can be tempting at this point to be satisfied with the epiphany that you are much more socially capable than you originally thought. However, this could just be an excuse to avoid testing your limits. Spend a period of time testing the limits of what you assume to be socially

acceptable. Obviously you shouldn't do something rude like slap someone in the face just because you find it funny. But you can say crazier things. You don't need to have high standards for what you say. They imply you care too much about what people think anyway. You can say ridiculous things because it makes you laugh.

Don't censor yourself. When you think of something you would enjoy saying or doing just do it! When you waste your time debating about whether you should do it or not you are just making yourself feel tired and reinforcing a negative mindset that makes you question if every action is good enough.

Be curious about other people and ask questions about their behavior nobody else is asking. When you don't get a fun response from others remember to accept it and that you don't need their reaction to feel good about yourself. You are doing this for you, not for them.

Accept Every Outcome No Matter What

When you self-amuse it's important to accept any outcome. For example you might think it's hilarious to answer the boring question *"What's your job?"* by saying you are a spy or a bank robber. Most people will in fact find this entertaining because they expect the usual boring answers to these standard questions.

You can jokingly roleplay how you are both spies for a moment, have a nice laugh, and if they are genuinely interested in the real answer you can inform them. Someday you might meet a very serious person with no sense of humor. They won't smile. They might even give a negative, rude reaction to your playfulness. But you shouldn't be affected because you didn't need it to feel good. You feel good because you are amusing yourself, not because you are trying to entertain others.

Instead of fearing potential outcomes become curious about them. The socially fearful survive by intentionally shrinking the size of their comfort zone to protect themselves from imagined dangers. They imagine all sorts of negative outcomes of social interactions.

They worry they might not have the right social skills, might blush, stutter or say something stupid. Their inability to achieve perfection in social interaction is a reminder of the pain of previous embarrassments and shame. They refuse to accept any reality that doesn't involve the entire world showering them with praise and love so they know they are worthy. As a result of their inability to control social reality, their social world can only constrict and get smaller.

When you let go of your need to control reality your social world will naturally expand. Instead of resisting the possibilities you embrace them. Instead of stings of rejection you feel gratitude that someone didn't waste your time pretending to be interested in you when they weren't.

Embracing the possibilities allows you to accept more fun, happiness and authenticity into your life. Without outcome dependency you are free to relax. Negative, needy desires for approval and certain outcomes will no longer inhibit your authenticity. This freedom allows you to finally amuse yourself in social situations and enjoy the process.

If you pay attention to interactions at parties, bars, and similar social events, you may realize it's often the people best at self-amusing who receive the most attention from others. This doesn't necessarily mean they are constantly teasing others and joking around with ridiculous statements. It simply means they are engaged with others without needing anything in return.

The self-amusement structure:

1. You get an idea! (Question, high five, staring contest, etc.)
2. You do it!
3. Accept the results no matter what!

Notice, between steps 1 and 2 there is no step where you waste time and energy on debating whether you should do it or not. If your former habits of self-doubt begin tempting you with the false comfort of avoidance you can tell that doubt to shut the hell up and just do it.

There should be no time in between steps one and two at all. You should instantly take action. If you start worrying about potential awkward outcomes you are no longer having fun! So it wouldn't be self-amusing when you finally do it because you care too much about the outcome!

A common mistake of the socially challenged is to reuse funny statements they heard someone use before. Maybe a confident guy says a humorous line and the shy guy sees this line received a lot of smiles and laughs from the group. The shy guy later uses this same line among a different group of people and gets zero reaction. His mistake is believing the line held some sort of magic to win people over. But the line wasn't crafted by years of rewriting until something socially potent was discovered. It came to the confident guy in the moment. As he is confident he doesn't care what the others in the group think of him. He doesn't carefully filter through all his thoughts to make sure they are always acceptable to everyone. In the moment he thought of the line, and then just as quickly spit it out to the amusement of himself and those around him.

Self-amused people are more likeable

The self-amused have more friends. They have a richer social life. They seem to possess endless charisma and social skills. They have a more satisfying dating life. They are better at interacting with coworkers. They are just more likeable and attractive.

When you think about it the reasons are clear. Though negative people may be drawn towards each other's toxic energy, their approval seeking behavior and outcome dependency can make them seem rather creepy and ends up pushing many people away.

Self-amusement is a display of outcome independence. It shows you aren't stifled by a socially anxious impulse to filter everything you say.

It shows you are authentic and not trying to hide any part of who you are. It is an indication that you are engaged with the present moment and happily being yourself. People are naturally drawn to this positivity and authenticity.

It is ironic how the people who most desperately wish to be liked are often the least likeable.

Their negative mindsets, needy behavior, and convoluted strategies to impress others often backfires as it only exposes their inauthenticity and insecurity.

Developing yourself to the point where you can self-amuse is therefore essential to social confidence.

How to Get Good at Self-Amusement

By now you understand the concept. However quite a few people learn about self-amusement but still claim they don't know what to say in social situations. To help you reeducate the filter between thought and action here are some effective tips.

Be curious.

When you start a conversation maybe you would like an enjoyable interaction, but you no longer need it. When you aren't dependent on a special outcome you are free to satisfy your curiosity. Take action simply to see what happens. Say silly things because you are curious how people will react. Will they be embarrassed? Excited? Offended? Happy? What does their reaction say about them? You can learn so much from these experiments.

When you are no longer in your head focused on how others are perceiving you it's possible to devote more attention to the environment and people around you. This means you will be more aware of things you can be curious about and comment on. No matter where you are or where you are doing, there will be plenty of conversation material available. When you are paying attention to what is happening around you it's easier to develop curiosity.

Stop Self-Censoring

Common sense prevents you from saying a lot of offensive thoughts that come to your mind. You know it wouldn't be nice to tell a stranger they are ugly. For the most part people seem to restrain their nasty thoughts. This socially conditioned politeness keeps us out of trouble.

However the socially anxious often over censor themselves. The only thoughts that get through the filter are those made to please others. Losing the approval of others would be too scary so they overcompensate by speaking very carefully. Self-amusement can't happen when you self-censor.

Prioritize Self-Amusement

If you had severe social anxiety before starting this program you may have been more concerned with how others thought about you than anything else. You may not have cared about enjoying social interactions because it was hard enough to start a conversation.

Now that you are making some progress and starting to practice self-amusement you can start to prioritize your own desire to enjoy the moment. You can start inviting people to do things you are interested in. You can start going to social events and saying whatever you find amusing with your new acquaintances. Your most rewarding experiences will happen when you are self-amused.

Self-amusement increases your own joy.

The Conversation

Do you worry about how to start conversations? Do you worry about saying the right thing? That worry is what will ruin your chances at building a connection with someone.

The best way to start a conversation is to assume the conversation is already started. This way there is no need to worry about how to start it. There is no reason to worry about what to say first. You don't need to agonize about what you will say. You can self-amuse if you want. Some phrases I like to use are:

"Hey who are you?"
"I guess you are a (some occupation)"
"Hey how was your day?"

These are of course just examples. You don't need to regurgitate these or any interesting lines you've encountered. Playfully say whatever you want.

After you've started the conversation by sharing your own positivity, hopefully they will reciprocate by expressing how self-amusing they can be as well. Everyone is capable of being interesting. You just need to use your curiosity to discover what is interesting about them.

If you realize someone really is incredibly boring then you don't need to keep the conversation going if you don't want to. Be aware that some people will chase your validation if you don't hand it out easily.

Have opinions

One of the biggest reasons guys claim to have nothing to add to conversations is that they don't care about anything. They are deficient in original thoughts. They are worried about having opinions that might make them outcasts so they blindly agree with the popular ideas of their community. They are lost in their inner world of seeking approval and avoiding awkwardness so they never have time to really think about anything else.

It's healthy to have high standards and think about what you like and dislike. When you watch a movie think about its meaning and whether you agree with it or not. Did any of the characters make choices you think are stupid? What is your honest opinion about popular music? Just as many people love it as hate it.

Form your own nuanced opinion instead of following what's popular.

Think about controversial topics. What are the popular opinions on these topics? Do you agree? Why or why not?

Read more books, especially about topics you are interested in.

If you usually eat at the same few restaurants start eating at new places and always try the most interesting looking items on the menu. Critique the presentation, flavor of the food, and overall atmosphere of the venue. Whenever you go to new places you can start forming opinions about the place. Ideally you will be more objective instead of constantly complaining, but at least you are forming your own ideas.

Get more life experience. Have some adventures. Go kayaking, bungee jumping, and other fun things you've always wanted to try. It's easier to have opinions about things you've been exposed to.

Now that you feel the freedom to self-amuse you can honestly share your opinions without fearing disagreement will mean nobody will ever like you.

Chapter 14: Confident Communication Skills

"I learned this, at least, by my experiment: that if one advances confidently in the direction of his dreams, and endeavors to live the life which he has imagined, he will meet with a success unexpected in common hours."
— <u>Henry David Thoreau</u>

To improve social confidence you need to work on both resolving internal issues and developing external skills. As explained several times already, when you combine deep introspection with action many bad habits will naturally dissolve.

Stutters, for example may feel a choking sensation in the throat when anxious. It's like the words hit a wall on the way out. The brain is getting mixed signals. Speak! Shut up! Speak! No don't speak it's scary! Speak! These confusing messages in the mind lead to awkward stifled behavior. But when you can accept yourself and your emotional responses there is no reason to resist the urge to say what you want to say. The stuttering would be greatly reduced as you aren't constantly battling between the urge to socialize and the urge to protect yourself from scrutiny.

You have likely had similar experiences. After a few friendly social interactions you were able to relax. With this relaxation many of your bad habits disappeared. You could laugh and enjoy talking with some new people. But in other situations people intimidated you. Then you felt stifled. You didn't know what to say. You felt judged. You worried about what people thought about you.

When you finally got the courage to speak the volume was too low and people asked you to repeat several times.

When you start to develop social confidence with the skills and methods of this book, at first you may still have trouble shaking off some bad habits. Or maybe you aren't aware of these habits at all. Depending on the severity of your social anxiety. This is why it can be helpful to record yourself and hear your own voice and see your own body language. It can be even more helpful to show these recordings of your social interactions to others and ask for their evaluation. If you trust someone enough to be honest with you, their real perspective could help you completely change how others see you.

Though many unconscious bad habits will disappear with social experience it can be helpful to make a conscious effort to develop better conversation skills. In this section we will discuss common habits of poor communication and how to fix them. Don't become paranoid if you are sometimes guilty of a few of these. This section isn't provided to make you worry about your lack of social skills. As mentioned, those skills come with practice. This section is meant to help you build awareness of habits you may need to change.

Nervous Laughter

Has someone ever made fun of you and you responded with laughter even though inside you felt at least a little hurt? This is a sign of trying to protect your ego. You want to make everyone think you are completely fine but inside you may be devastated to lose the approval of someone you respected.

Nervous laughter is a fake attempt at masking internal pain. This doesn't mean you have to cry like a baby when someone hurts your feelings. But it does mean you might want to look at your motivations for putting up a false front. Why do you care about making people think you haven't been emotionally impacted?

Silence

The opposite of nervous laughter is silence. When some people face intimidation or fearful situations they close up. They aren't able to say anything. When they do try to speak they can't say much because every cell in the body is urging them to run away.

To fix this requires facing fears and actively verbalizing your real thoughts and feelings. When you are scared to share what you are really thinking that is exactly the time to practice expressing yourself.

Mumbling

Mumblers speak softly and with poor enunciation. Words blend into each other quickly, or are completely left out of sentences. The first part of the sentences may take place only in the mumbler's head before it is finished in a barely audible mess of words.

If people often ask you to repeat yourself, you might occasionally mumble instead of speaking clearly and with authority. When you mumble it shows you aren't confident enough to loudly and directly state exactly what you want to say. It could also mean you are hiding what you want to say. You want to share it, but you are afraid of people's reactions so can't let it all out.

Fix this by practicing speaking loudly and clearly in front of a mirror. Notice how you form words. Some people are afraid of using the full range of their vocal power. Open your mouth widely and enunciate every syllable of each word. Try to speak with the same volume and clarity throughout each sentence.

Next you can try practicing enunciation when you go about your daily errands. When you speak to shop clerks and other people intentionally speak as clearly as possible. With practice people should pay more attention to your speaking.

Conversation Fillers

These are words such as "um, ah, yeah, like." They often come out more frequently when someone is nervous and feels pressured to say something. I had a history professor in college who often used filler words in class. He seemed to easily get nervous. One day he gave a speech in front of an audience of a few hundred students. I happened to be there and before he began speaking I easily predicted his speech would be filled with these fillers. I was right. Nearly every other word was a shaky "um." Or "uh."

Fix these by paying attention to how you speak. When you realize you are about to let out a meaningless sound out of nervousness replace it with a deep breath instead and accept the silence. Don't worry about always having something to say. Silence can have a much bigger impact on a conversation anyway. As you take a deep breathe you can calmly formulate your next thought.

Speed and Voice

Often when you are too nervous you try to get words out quickly before you can be interrupted. It shows you aren't confident people would want to listen to your words.

Social anxiety can also limit the vocal range of your voice and leave you speaking with an annoying high pitch. Lower, deeper voices are more persuasive and command more attention.

To fix this first realize you are trying to speak too fast. Record yourself speaking or reading. Pay attention to how you sound and make adjustments.

Remember, most of these are a result of deep internal fear of inadequacy. They are only symptoms but not the disease. Though you may find great advice to change a few of these habits, that internal fear will still be there if you never face it. By handling the internal pain you will strengthen yourself and eliminate the source of many poor communication habits indicative of low confidence. Remaining poor communication skills can only be blamed on a bad habit that could be changed with effort.

Confident Communication Skills

Much of this should come naturally when you are in a social mood and communicating without any ulterior motives besides enjoying the act of expressing yourself. However this section offers helpful tips for developing confident communication skills.

Engaging Questions

When socializing there are only 3 known options to communicate:

1. Ask a question
2. Make a comment
3. Nonverbal actions

Nonverbal actions could be making eye contact, smiling, and waving at someone before gesturing for them to come talk to you. Making a comment is often recommended over asking questions because a comment implies you aren't married to getting a response back. It's an indication of non-neediness so some guys scared of exposing their needy vibe are careful not to ask too many questions. Asking a question is only a problem when you don't actually care about the answer.

When you ask a question genuinely engage with the person you are asking. The boring interview questions everyone asks only scratch the surface of what you could find out about every person.

"Where are you from?"

"What's your job?"

"How old are you?"

"How long have you lived here?"

"Do you like the weather here?"

These questions are all common and acceptable. Hopefully they lead to opportunities to really connect with and learn from others. Unfortunately they are painfully boring. Eventually you need to get to questions that are really interesting for you. To do this, find out what is interesting about each person you interact with.

Ask everything you want to know. Your inner dialogue may resist. You might think it's too personal, not relevant to a current topic, or too sudden. But realize these are just excuses.

When you only ask the boring, safe to ask questions you encourage people to keep up a superficial shield of politeness. This discourages authenticity. When you finally find the courage to ask exactly what you want to it gets people to open up. You will finally have an opportunity to build a genuine connection.

A client of mine recently started a conversation with a girl he saw in a book store. She was looking at a book so he asked her if she liked adventure novels. They talked for about a minute about books but then he couldn't think of anything to ask except boring small talk questions. He excused himself and finished the conversation even though he wanted to get to know her more.

To fix this he could have asked himself, "What am I most curious about?" or "What do I really want to know about this person?" He said he wanted to know why a girl who dressed so feminine was interested in action novels. He wanted to know if she liked fighting or other physical activities. He wanted to know if most of her friends were men who influenced her to like manly interests. These are all great topics of conversation. He could have guessed, "How does someone with such feminine fashion get to like such manly books?" It's a fun observational statement that shows interest in getting to know her.

If he wanted to know these things, then why didn't he ask? Because he was more concerned with keeping the conversation going and keeping her attention than in actually getting to know her. If you are detached from the outcome and genuinely curious about someone the conversation can flow for hours without you even realizing how much time has passed.

When you talk to people, what are you really interested in? Those are the things you should be asking about.

Here are some possibilities:

- Hobbies
- Musical talents
- Sense of humor
- Passions
- Goals
- Fetishes
- Relationships
- How someone treats others
- Favorite movies, music and books
- Secrets
- Special skills
- What they do for fun
- Their childhood

- Accomplishments they are proud of
- Places they want to go
- Things they want to do
- Skills they want to learn
- Embarrassing moments
- Kinds of people they like
- Kinds of people they hate
- Kinds of people they'd like to date/marry
- Famous people they'd like to meet
- Mistakes they've learned from

These are just a handful of examples. In reality there are unlimited possibilities. With just that list you could keep a conversation going with anyone for hours. Everyone has opinions and life experience with these topics. If you can get people to share their real thoughts you can break through that wall of politeness.

Think about what really interests you and ask related questions. If you want to know about someone's goals you could ask questions like:

"What exciting things are you working on now?"

"What do you plan to be doing 10 years from now?"

Or even bluntly ask, "So what are your goals in life?"

You can ask these questions to anyone. When they respond they will provide even more areas for you to be curious about. So you can ask even more follow up questions. Listen and pay attention. There is always something to talk about.

If you are stuck in your head worrying about what your next question will be you might miss the amazing response they gave you and kill the conversation because you were so worried about messing up.

Sharing

Sharing information about yourself can be uncomfortable for the socially anxious. It can seem like any bit of information you provide could be judged so might as well hold back as much as possible. But this resistance to sharing is another wall that puts distance between yourself and others. Without sharing the conversation will eventually stop.

If someone is open to sharing their information to you, but realize you won't do the same they will feel you are closed off to making a connection.

Let's say a coworker or classmate asks you, "How was your weekend?" Many people may take this question as just a polite greeting and not really feel the need to provide the details of their awesome weekend.

But what if you actually shared the story? You might worry some people would be bored with what you have to say. So you only respond with the usual, "Not bad."

If the only reason you are selective about who you open up to is your fear of what others think of you then it's time to face that fear. It's time to finally practice sharing more information about yourself. Instead of only saying, "Not bad," you could add a detail about something you did.

This would give the other person something to comment on fuel the conversation.

The interaction could look closer to this:

"How was your weekend?"

"Not bad. I went on a short trip to ____."

"Oh how was that? I haven't been there yet."

The other person now has a bit of info to comment on and keep a conversation going. People often assume others aren't interested in what they have to say so withhold information.

If you have negative assumptions like this you only reinforce a negative assessment of your ability to engage people in conversation.

You also constantly miss opportunities to share your passions and practice speaking in a way that would generate interest no matter the topic.

If you assume your life is more boring than a speck of paint everything you say will reflect this negative belief.

You could actually have some interesting hobbies but worry they aren't interesting enough to talk about. Your interests don't need to be so unique. It could be video games, going to the gym or whatever it is you are into.

The problem is people are so worried about gaining the approval of others they are afraid their interests aren't good enough. They worry if they have the wrong interests they could lose the approval of others. This lack of confidence comes through in how you communicate.

If someone asks, "What do you do for fun?" How do you answer?

Shy people might quietly say something like, "Nothing special, just normal stuff like watching movies and listening to music."

I hate this answer because it's so unoriginal. It's too safe because most people watch movies and listen to music. Unless you are seriously passionate about movies or are a musician you can always think of a more original answer.

The shy guy might actually be an accomplished artist. With confidence he could answer the same question by saying, "Actually I love painting nature scenes. I've been working on a mural of an eagle hunting a deer on my wall lately."

By saying it this way he is speaking with passion. But he's worried this answer isn't cool enough, or is too weird, so he's not confident enough in the truth to say it. It is the passion in your voice that engages people more than the topic.

Have you ever had a teacher in school whose voice was monotone and extremely boring? Maybe the content of the class was actually really interesting.

History is actually full of fascinating stories for example. But if your history teacher has no passion for the topic you'll tune out. Conversely, it's possible you had a teacher who taught with passion for a topic you originally found boring. He may have inspired you to actually be fascinated by this topic.

It is therefore your passion to speak about what interests you that engages people. If you aren't confident in what you have to say, other people will show similar disinterest. This is why it's important to share instead of withhold your real opinions and interests. By holding back information about yourself you only prevent connection.

When you filter what you say it can make people uncomfortable to share their own information. As the saying goes, treat people how you want to be treated. By sharing what matters to you it's easier to get other people to open up and easier to find people who appreciate your interests.

You can't predict how people will react to what you say. There is no reason to try to control it. Just share what you want to say.

Insecure people are worried about maintaining a front of perfection. They worry about sharing anything in their life they haven't handled yet because it would highlight their flaws. People who don't want to share are often stuck in these negative mindsets because they worry too much about being judged.

With inner work, it will become easier. However it still takes conscious effort to honestly share what is going on in your life. Once you start sharing you will find your conversations became much richer and enjoyable.

Socially Confident Behavior

Let's compare confident behavior with indications of low self-confidence. By now these differences should be familiar to you. However actually making the decision to engage in the highly confident behavior can take some effort if you have a habit of nervously avoiding some social interactions.

High Confidence: Doing what you believe what is right, even if others criticize you for it. This could be something potentially embarrassing like the rejection challenge, or talking to people you know you want to meet.

Low Confidence: Basing one's behavior and personality on what other people will accept. Of course living in a human society there are rules of common sense, and laws meant to keep us from annoying and harming each other. With that said there is still an immense amount of room for freedom of expression. Which is why it's a tragedy so many people never let figure out who they really are.

High Confidence: Willingness to take risks to achieve as much as possible. The highly confident aren't afraid of failure. Failure doesn't devastate their self-esteem. It is only a learning opportunity. Confident people can afford to take risks. Their identity isn't tied up in a superficial desire to maintain an outward appearance of perfection. Even if they don't get what they want it doesn't matter because eventually they will succeed.

Low Confidence: Afraid of taking risks, staying in the comfort zone.

High Confidence: Owning up to your mistakes and learning from them. Mistakes are learning opportunities. If you've called someone by the wrong name just admit it and make an effort to use the correct name. Some severely anxious people might view this forgettable error with more seriousness than it's worth and feel embarrassed for the rest of the day.

Low Confidence: Trying to hide mistakes and hoping no one notices. It's probably better to tell people about your mistakes and deal with the consequences.

High Confidence: Not needing praise for successes.

Low Confidence: Bragging about anything. Hoping to win the approval of others.

High Confidence: Starting a conversation expecting a socially intelligent reaction, but not getting upset if it doesn't happen.

Low Confidence: Starting a conversation and needing a good reaction to feel better about yourself.

High Confidence: Self amusement. Saying things because you find it entertaining not because you are seeking a reaction.

Low Confidence: Hiding your real thoughts or saying something odd just for the attention.

High Confidence: Making suggestions and decisions. Such as where to stand, sit, go to eat, etc. Confident people can lead interactions and expects their suggestions to be followed.

It doesn't mean you need to tyrannically enforce your will at every opportunity. You can still openly debate the options. It just means you are capable of asserting your desires.

Low Confidence: Always following and agreeing with others no matter what. Never challenging a plan they don't actually like.

As you interact with others you will find yourself in crucial moments where you need to decide if you will behave with high confidence or low confidence. You already know which behaviors are high confidence and which are low. The only thing preventing you from taking the confident action is the impulse to avoid imagined danger. Whenever this happens remember to remind yourself to sit with that feeling and accept it. Acknowledge that nothing terrible has actually happened and stop worrying about what others think about you. It's not something you can control anyway. With practice making the correct choice gets easier until you naturally respond with confidence.

Chapter 15: Your 10 Day Social Confidence Plan

"Let your plans be dark and impenetrable as night, and when you move, fall like a thunderbolt."
— Sun Tzu, The Art of War

Mastering social confidence will take commitment. Your fears and social inhibitions won't dissolve instantly, but you can make progress in even a short amount of time if you follow the advice presented in this book.

This chapter will review Social Confidence Mastery and present a basic 10 day plan for implementing these methods. 10 days was chosen because the more days we add the more people resist even starting. Also, it is definitely possible to feel more confident within a few consecutive days of confronting both internal and external fears. If the presented plan isn't challenging enough for you then add more days, more challenges and longer practice sessions. This is a template to help you formulate the most effective plan for yourself.

Choose a day to start. The sooner the better. You want to live confidently so might as well start facing your fears.

The plan asks you to immerse yourself in 10 days of social interactions. Look up local events, and parties in your area. You can also look up interesting meetups on meetup.com. Ideally you could find a social event for every day in your 10 day Social Confidence Mastery Plan. However if several days don't happen to have any events you are interested in, it is not an excuse to avoid socializing. Find a place with people around and force yourself to talk to people.

Day 0

1. Remind yourself of your goals. If you haven't done so yet, absolutely write them down. Envision the social life and confidence you want in your life. What steps do you need to take to turn that into reality?

2. What benefits do you want from improving your confidence? How does your fearful avoidant behavior prevent your life from improving in the ways you want? Answering these two questions helps to remind you of the cost of remaining in your comfort zone and the rewards for stepping out of it and reprogramming your mind.

3. As you prepare to begin this 10 day transformation process, how do you feel? Excited? Nervous? Are avoidant thoughts tempting you to not even try? Sit down in a comfortable position and close your eyes as you concentrate on these feelings. Use the Body Mindfulness Meditation we used in the chapter on overcoming anxious feelings. Accept your feelings. Accept the avoidant thoughts and follow them to their source. Maintain your commitment to your

personalized 10 Day Social Confidence Mastery Plan.

4. Rewrite your limiting beliefs. Which of the tasks in your plan do you not yet feel comfortable enough to attempt? Write these down and remind yourself of what you gain by facing these fears. Widen your comfort zone a little each day. Your tasks should gradually become more challenging for you. On day one your day 10 tasks should involve something you don't believe you have the confidence to attempt. But by day 9 you should start believing it is possible even if you still feel some anxiety about it.

Day 1

1. **Practice confident body language from Chapter 2.**
   Remind yourself to maintain eye contact, confident posture, and to speak clearly and loudly enough for people nearby to hear what you say. It can be helpful to review the advice of Chapter 2 today.

2. **Start immersing yourself in social situations**
   Go to at least one social event or venue. This will help you get into a social mood. If you socialize every day the momentum will build and it will feel more natural to talk to anyone.

3. **Start 10 Days of Rejection Therapy**
   By now you should have 10 requests prepared. One for each of the next 10 days. Remember you must get rejected at least once a day. If you aren't rejected it doesn't count and you need to add an extra day of rejection after your 10 days. You must be out of your comfort zone and making the request can't be easy for you.

Example: Ask someone if you can have a piece of gum.

4. **Balance Imbalances**

    Review chapter 5 and your notes about personality traits you may be overcompensating for. In case you haven't yet memorized the process, here it is again for your convenience:

Step 1:

Choose the area in which you may be overcompensating for disowned traits. Such as if you are a very quiet person maybe overly talkative people make you uncomfortable. This suggests you've rejected the talkative/expressive part of yourself.

Choose a person or situation that irritates or upsets you in relation to this trait. Perhaps a relative or coworker is too chatty or has some other behavior that triggers a strong emotional reaction within you.

Step 2:

Visualize this person and pinpoint the details that upset you the most. Write down your emotions or at least discuss them with yourself

Step 3:

Change the memory. Talk to the person whose actions upset you as if they were actually present. Tell them exactly what you want to say.

Ask them questions such as these:

- Why are you doing that?
- What do you want?
- Why do you behave differently than I would in the same situation?
- What can I learn from this?

Allow your imagination to provide answers to your questions. It will be even more effective if you record this conversation in writing.

Step 4:

Pretend you've traded places with this person and you see things from their perspective. See the situation as they see it. Ask yourself questions to figure out the motivations of this perspective. Why do you shout angrily? Answers will emerge from your imagination.

Describe yourself in this new perspective:

- I am loud
- I am angry.
- I am rude

The more uncomfortable this is the more you have likely disowned these traits.

Step 5:

Acknowledge these disowned traits in yourself. Remember specific experiences in which you have felt and behaved in the same ways as the people who upset you. Accept that this same trait does actually exist within you too. Don't be ashamed of it. Accept it and even find something pleasurable in exploring this side of yourself. This will allow you to re-own it.

5. **Record your day**
   Keep a journal of your experiences throughout the day.
   How did it feel to go to the social event?
   Did you start conversations?
   How did it go?
   How was the rejection challenge? Was it easier than you expected?
   How do you feel now?

Day 2

1. **Rejection Therapy 2**
   Example: Challenge a stranger to arm wrestle

2. **Build Social momentum**
   Go to another social event or venue and practice using the advice of Chapter 3 to get into a social mood without relying on alcohol:
   I. Keep talking to new people
   II. Minimize time between interactions
   III. Don't let uncomfortable experiences prevent more interactions.
   IV. Stay present to the moment.

3. **Balance Imbalances**
   Continue balancing anything you may have rejected within yourself. Practice self-compassion and acceptance. Spend at least 10 minutes on this.

4. **Record your day.**
   Was it difficult to practice social momentum?
   What feelings did you have?

What did you try to avoid?
Congratulate yourself on your progress and prepare for the next day.

Day 3

1. **Rejection Therapy 3**
   Example: Ask someone if they like your shoes.

2. **Balance Imbalances**
   Spend at least one hour focused on accepting every part of yourself. Accept every fear, desire, and shameful thought.
   Accept any painful memories that arise. You can do this laying down if you want. Don't worry if your mind wanders as long as you remind yourself to refocus on what's important.

3. **Social Momentum**
   Go to yet another social event and practice socializing with as many people as possible. Remember you don't need anything from anyone.

4. **Record your day.**
   Was anything easier today?

Day 4

1. **Rejection Therapy 4**
   Example: Ask someone if they have any good jokes

2. **Ask engaging questions and share.**
   Go to another social event or venue and ask the questions you are really interested in. Find out what is interesting about each person you talk to. Also share your own stories and opinions about yourself.

3. **Body Mindfulness Meditation**
   Think about your experiences of the day. At which points did you feel nervous or uncomfortable?

To help you practice accepting these feelings and learning from them use the Body Mindfulness Meditation from Chapter 6: Accepting Anxious Feelings. Here it's repeated for your convenience:

Part 1:

Sit in a comfortable position with your back straight. Take 10 deep breaths one after the other. Inhale quickly. Exhale normally. If you must you can lay down at this point. Avoid moving as much as possible.

With your eyes closed start paying attention to your breathing. Breathe normally. Don't control it. Just experience it. Notice how your body expands on the inhale and contracts on the exhale.

Next move your awareness to your toes. Spend a moment on that spot before concentrating on the entire foot. Slowly move awareness up the body as you go. How does that part of the body feel? Warm, cool, sore, stiff, itchy, etc.

Spend a few breaths on each part of your body before shifting awareness. If you have recently been feeling social anxiety try to find where that emotion is located in your body. If it is uncomfortable to accept these negative feelings it will require practice.

Part 2: Accepting Anxious Feelings

I. What sensations do you feel when you encounter social situations you are afraid of? Examples may be dry mouth, sweating, racing heart rate, shaking, blushing, chest discomfort, a choking sensation in the throat preventing you from speaking etc.

II. Accept these sensations. Remember any anxiety inducing situations you encountered today. What sensations do you feel and where? Accept these sensations. If this becomes too intense you can take a break and continue the next day. Let go of urges to ignore or change these uncomfortable feelings.

4. **Record your experiences.**
When you encounter social anxiety what do you feel and where?
How is your progress to accepting these sensations instead of resisting them?
Did you still feel like avoiding any interactions? If so why?

Day 5

1. **Rejection Therapy 5**
   Example: Go to a fast food restaurant and ask a stranger for a French fry.

2. **Engaging Questions and Sharing.**
   Today share even more of your own thoughts and experiences with others. Share your passion for everything you talk about.

3. **Body Mindfulness Meditation.**
   Pay attention to what is going on in your body. When you socialize and have enjoyable interactions do you feel anything different?

4. **Record Your Experiences.**

Day 6

1. **Rejection Therapy Day 6**
   Example: In a public sitting area, ask someone to give you their seat.

2. **Give More than You Take.**
   Go to another social event or venue and get into a social mood. Focus on sharing your value, passion and happiness with others. Intentionally talk to people without wanting anything in return. You don't need them to give you good reactions. You don't need the phone number of that cute girl. You are happy to share your value.

3. **Body Mindfulness Meditation.**
   Pay attention to what is going on in your body. When you socialize and have enjoyable interactions do you feel anything different?

4. **Record Your Experiences.**

Day 7

1. **Rejection Therapy 7**
   Example: Ask someone to guess your favorite color

2. **Self-Amusement.**
   Go to a social event or venue and practice amusing yourself by expressing exactly what you want to say and do. Don't worry if someone doesn't appreciate what you have to say. You aren't trying to impress anyone. You don't need their opinions to feel good about yourself. You are self-amused. Self-amusement is best expressed in the moment. So when you think of something funny to say or do you absolutely must do it.

3. **Meditation.**
   Spend at least 10 minutes in silent meditation. The only goal is to accept whatever thoughts and feelings arise and then to let them go.

4. **Record Your Experiences.**
   How was your attempt at self-amusement?
   How was the meditation?
   Are you making progress with accepting rejection?

Day 8

5. Rejection Therapy 8
Example: Ask a stranger if you can take a picture with them.

6. Self-Amusement.
Go to a social event or venue and practice amusing yourself by expressing exactly what you want to say and do. Don't worry if someone doesn't appreciate what you have to say. You aren't trying to impress anyone. You don't need their opinions to feel good about yourself. You are self-amused. Self-amusement is best expressed in the moment. So when you think of something funny to say or do you absolutely must do it.

7. Meditation.
Spend at least 15 minutes in silent meditation. Don't move for anything. You can set an alarm for this if you want.

8. Record Your Experiences.
How was your attempt at self-amusement? How was the meditation?

Day 9

1. **Rejection Therapy 9**
   Example: Ask an attractive stranger, "Hey can I talk to you?"
   This is only an example and you are free to choose any rejection requests you think of that put you out of your comfort zone. It's not recommended you ask this question if you really are interested in someone because the subtext is you think aren't good enough for them to want to talk to you. However accepting this possible rejection is a vital step to maturity and social confidence so I've included it here as a possibility.

2. **Self-Amusement.**
   Go to a social event or venue and practice amusing yourself by expressing exactly what you want to say and do. Don't worry if someone doesn't appreciate what you have to say. You aren't trying to impress anyone. You don't need their opinions to feel good about yourself. You are self-amused. Self-amusement is best expressed in the moment. So when you think of something funny to say or do you absolutely must do it.

3. **Meditation.**
   Spend at least 20 minutes in silent meditation. Don't move for anything. Observe your thoughts and feelings. You can set an alarm for this if you want.

4. **Record Your Experiences.**
   How was your attempt at self-amusement?
   How was the meditation?
   Are you making progress with accepting rejection?

Day 10

1. **Rejection Therapy 10**
   Example: Go to a restaurant and ask for something that isn't on the menu.

2. **Self-Amusement.**
   Go to a social event or venue and practice amusing yourself by expressing exactly what you want to say and do. Don't worry if someone doesn't appreciate what you have to say. You aren't trying to impress anyone. You don't need their opinions to feel good about yourself. You are self-amused. Self-amusement is best expressed in the moment. So when you think of something funny to say or do you absolutely must do it.

   If you have been joking around a lot try to be more engaging and really get to know people this time. Tone down the humor a bit. If you are still nervous about saying something too ridiculous then give it a try this time.

3. **Invite people out**
   Plan an event. Go eat something, play a sport or some other fun activity you enjoy.

Call the venues and reserve places for your group. Invite the people you have been meeting the past 10 days.

4. **Meditation.** Spend at least 20 minutes in silent meditation. Try to not move for any reason. Set a timer if needed.

5. **Record the day.**
   How was your attempt at self-amusement?
   How was the meditation?
   Are you making progress with accepting rejection?

Congratulations!

You've finished your 10 day Social Confidence Mastery plan. If you bought this book with the intention of improving your social life, then you have actually taken action and started your own 10 day plan to face your fears and develop your social confidence.

If you didn't actually spend the bare minimum of 10 days on the methods in this book then there is no point complaining that it didn't work for you.

10 days won't necessarily change your life but it can demonstrate your own potential for enjoying social situations and expressing yourself.

As you go about life it should be easier to practice asserting yourself and accepting the occasional rejection. You should be able to recognize that true happiness and subsequently confidence comes from within, not from external validation.

Chapter 16: Conclusion

"You are never dedicated to something you have complete confidence in. No one is fanatically shouting that the sun is going to rise tomorrow. They know it's going to rise tomorrow. When people are fanatically dedicated to political or religious faiths or any other kinds of dogmas or goals, it's always because these dogmas or goals are in doubt."
— Robert M. Pirsig, Zen and the Art of Motorcycle Maintenance

Hopefully this book has helped convince you to stretch out the perimeter of your comfort zone. Facing fears is proven to be an effective way to build situational confidence. It's important, but it isn't sustainable by itself. Feelings of invincibility would be temporary. This is because you would need to constantly reinforce the belief in your confidence.

If you spend a few months giving speeches to large audiences every day, eventually it won't trigger any stage fright. By the last day you would be able to jump on stage with hardly any planning and deliver a creative message the audience would love. But if you then wait a year before giving another speech that fear will suddenly return.

Why is that?

It's because you recently have no environmental stimulus reminding you of your ability to give quality speeches. When you were giving daily speeches you had the immediate reference of the previous day's amazing speech. You could look back on your recent memories and believe today's effort would be just as successful.

However, if you then spent a year giving no speeches and speaking to hardly anyone you would not feel ready. Even if you typed out an excellent speech and memorized it, that fear would still linger.

There would be no recent references to convince you of your ability to deliver a great speech.

So should we constantly face every fear in a paranoid effort to avoid ever feeling it again?

You could try…

But no matter what you do eventually you will return to a fearful state. You would need to constantly demonstrate your confidence to yourself or you wouldn't believe it. You would constantly chase confidence but never catch it.

The solution is to rediscover the happiness and confidence already present within you. This allows you to give up the chase for confidence and happiness in every situation.

Some shy guys devote years building confidence in bars and night clubs. Their brains are conditioned to enjoy the moment in these specific venues. They can tap into their creativity because in these nightlife scenarios they've conditioned themselves to turn off the filter and avoidant behavior. Other people in these venues assume they are naturally charismatic and extremely confident. However the truth is in other situations, at work for example, they aren't as talkative or confident. Coworkers may ask questions but they still follow avoidant impulses and finish conversations as quickly as possible. They haven't yet made an effort to build confidence in other social situations.

Many books promote the benefits of facing fears to conquer them. Though on the surface it is very effective, it is not the only key to permanent change.

On a scale of 1 to 10 most people's emotional wellbeing and confidence may hover around 4 or 5. When they have enjoyable social interactions they feel their confidence shoot up a few points to 8 or more. But as soon as those experiences become mere memories, most people are back to the 4 or 5 baseline they are used to.

External validation can only raise your emotional state and confidence temporarily. Internal validation provides a more permanent increase in self-esteem. Once you've dealt with a majority of your negative internal baggage, started practicing self-acceptance and facing fears, this combination leads to a more sustainable solution to developing social confidence.

Those processes help you reestablish internal validation. This however doesn't mean external validation holds zero power over you. You still need to make a conscious effort to balance these two forces.

Some so-called self-help gurus advise you to accept everything the universe throws at you no matter how horrific. This is a profound theory. However to apply it you would need to be at a level of either maturity or psychopathy most people in the world are far from achieving. No matter how many hours a day you meditate you know how devastating the loss of a loved one could be for example.

As difficult as it can be to admit it, suffering helps you grow. Maturity comes with accepting what the universe throws at you. That doesn't mean you approve of the horrors people inflict on you and each other. It only means you acknowledge the reality that they exist.

You aren't powerless against external influences and social conditioning. You aren't just a chunk of driftwood beaten and thrown around by waves until you disintegrate. You have the power to choose the course you take. You have the power to accept stormy weather and use it as a catalyst for growth.

Ultimately it's up to you to decide if you want to invest in a plan that could finally diminish fear and improve your ability to express yourself.

Social confidence isn't a skill to be mimicked. You can't fake it till you make it because you would always be faking. Instead, share your authenticity until you remember who you really are.

Self-confidence means you accept your authentic self and don't need people to tell you who to be.

Pay attention to your emotions. They are tools to discovering your authenticity. They help you realize what attachments control your life. Such as an attachment (addiction) to the internet. If you waste all day looking at clickbait and pointless videos and then suddenly have a day with no internet access you might feel anxiety and discomfort. Your attachment to the internet began to control your behavior. Any time your attachments are threatened it can hurt.

Negative emotions are clues to identifying unhealthy attachments. People become addicted to routines and roles they play. When these routines and roles are threatened people may erupt in anger, become defensive, or avoid others. These unhelpful reactions block authenticity.

These negative reactions are caused by fear. Primarily the fear of losing social approval and love. We all want to be loved. The problem is, most love, attention, and approval is conditional. Even love between parents and children. Usually the mother still loves her son if he misbehaves and she shouts at him. However her love doesn't mean she has to allow him to do whatever he wants. As a parent she must encourage him to do the right thing. But it isn't obvious to the child. When his mother angrily demands he listen to what she wants, he only hears that conforming to his mother's wishes is the only way to continue to receive her love and affection. He is threatened with the loss of approval. He feels his survival depends on doing everything she says whether she demands it with the promise of reward or the threat of punishment.

Throughout our lives most relationships are conditional. A girl enjoys dating her boyfriend until he kisses another girl. Some people love hanging out when you are in a good mood but ignore you as soon as you feel bad about anything. They only want good emotions from you. Friends trust each other until someone is caught in an embarrassing lie. Employers pay you because you sell your life energy to them.

Your behavior can be conditional. You don't need to be friends with people who betray your trust. You can still learn from your mistakes but they don't need to devastate your emotional state.

When you do feel intense negative emotions, ask yourself, "Why do I feel like this?" When you trace the reasoning back far enough you often discover a reason based on a threat to a source of conditional love & approval.

For example, a man is angry at his roommate for making a little noise late at night.

Why?

Because he wants to sleep well.

Why?

Because he has a meeting tomorrow and he wants to be able to impress a cute new staff member. If he is too tired he won't feel mentally prepared to socialize.

When you have negative responses ask yourself, "What am I actually afraid of?"

Get to the cause of your fears and you can learn valuable lessons about yourself that help you reestablish the bond with authenticity.

Social anxiety is a more obvious example. We hope to be liked and we assume we need to flawlessly interact with others to win their approval. It reinforces the false belief that love, approval, attention, and respect should always be conditional.

When you are frustrated at your inability to start conversations with people you want to meet ask yourself "why?"

More often than not you will realize reasons such as:

"I'm worried no one will like me."

"I'm worried people won't listen to me."

"I'm worried something awkward will happen and I won't know what to do"

These thoughts all indicate fear of losing conditional approval. We think we need to speak perfectly and never stutter or mispronounce words to be loved by others. It isn't true. We think we need to be hilarious and charming to win their affection. It isn't true. We think we need to fearlessly engage others and constantly prove how confident we are. This too, is completely false.

When you put conditions on yourself to gain the approval and love of others you close yourself off from authenticity and happiness.

This authenticity is what is implied by the cliché "just be yourself." An overused but profound statement that is often misunderstood. Of course you should be yourself. But there may be decades of emotional baggage blocking the path from the mask you show the world to who you really are. Since we can't flip a switch and erase that baggage the next best approach is to clean up the pollution blocking your development. The tools of this book can help begin that process.

It is now up to you to decide when to begin. Hopefully when you read that sentence instead of the impulse to avoid social confrontation you feel excitement and enthusiasm to finally start living.

Thanks For Reading!

I hope this book has provided inspiration to face your fears and develop social confidence.

If you learned something from this book it will be helpful if you can write a review on Amazon.com so other people can benefit from your experiences.

Thanks again and I wish you sincere success with all your goals.

FREE BOOK!

If you haven't yet gotten your free copy of **100 Books Every Man Should Read** then download it now!

It covers the best books in every area important to men's self-development. Such as relationships, social skills, leadership, philosophy, and much more.

Go to Evolvetowin.com to get your free copy now.

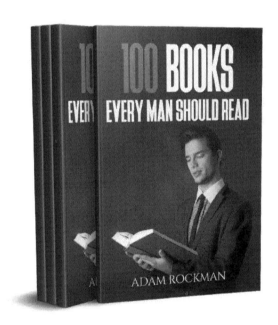

Other Books by the Author

10 Days to Superhuman Confidence: Cure Social Anxiety, Destroy Doubt, and Live Fearlessly

"I have read several books about confidence recently and this is definitely the best one. It's like the author was able to read my mind and dissect exactly what was holding me back! I followed the advice of this book and realize what I originally assumed to be confidence, was actually a fragile pride in limited success.
I've wasted too much time trying to please everyone when I should actually be trying to first satisfy my own needs and goals and then ideally using what I learn to contribute to the world."

— Candi A. Slocum

Other Books by the Author

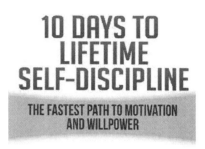

10 Days to Lifetime Self-Discipline: The Fastest Path to Motivation and Willpower

"Procrastination has always been my problem. After reading this book, I forced myself to go to the gym. I bought a subscription for a year. I feel the power to be able to beat my fat belly."

— Vasiliy

Other Books By the Author

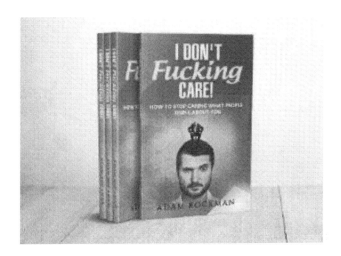

I Don't Fucking Care! : How to Stop Caring What People Think About You

"This book, hit me hard on the head and made me realize a lot of things I need to improve. I need to learn to love and appreciate myself first and just stop caring what other people think of me because in reality, they don't really care. What's important is how I see myself. Loved this book!"

— Lotte

Social Confidence Mastery

How to Eliminate Social Anxiety, Insecurities, Shyness, and the Fear of Rejection

By Adam Rockman

WWW.EVOLVETOWIN.COM

Made in the USA
San Bernardino, CA
20 March 2019